RESURRECTION
FACT OR FICTION

A Trial Lawyer Examines All of the Evidence

RESURRECTION
FACT OR FICTION
A Trial Lawyer Examines All of the Evidence

Part I:
- LIFE'S TWO QUESTIONS
- PROTECT YOUR CHILDREN
- THE ISIS CRISIS & The Covid-19 Pandemic
- FREE WILL & FREEDOM
- MEANING OF LIFE
- PREJUDICE AND EQUALITY
- CHRISTIAN EXCLUSIVITY
- CHRISTIAN CHRONOLOGY
- GOSPEL FACTS

Part II:
REASON FOR OUR HOPE:
Undeniable Proof of Our Creator God

Part III:
LIFE'S REALITY PLAY

Note: If you read - and teach your children - only one book other than the Bible, make it this one!

Wilbur McCoy Otto

Resurrection—Fact or Fiction: A trial Lawyer Examines all of the Evidence

This book is written to provide information and motivation to readers. Its purpose is not to render any type of psychological, legal, or professional advice of any kind. The content is the sole opinion and expression of the author, and not necessarily that of the publisher.

ARPress
45 Dan Road Suite 36
Canton MA 02021

Hotline: 1(888) 821-0229
Fax: 1(508) 545-7580

Ordering Information:
Quantity Sales. Special discounts are available on quantity purchases by corporations, associations, and others. For details, contact the publisher at the address above.

Printed in the United States of America.

ISBN-13   Softcover   979-8--89356-924-7
              eBook   979-889356-925-4

Library of Congress Control Number: 2024905903

Contents

Dedication ix
Acknowledgements...xi
Forward...xiii

PART I. Resurrection: Fact or Fiction

Chapter 1: World Crises...2
    Ishmael v. Isaac 2
    Warning of 9/11 4
    Covid-19 Pandemic 5
    Are Your Children and Grandchildren Safe?...6
    The Two Most Important Questions in Every Human's Life.........................7
    The Centrality of the Issue of the Resurrection of Jesus Christ 8

Chapter 2: Key World Facts, Circumstances, and Status.......................................9
    Calendar Dating 9
    Christianity...9
    Pre-Resurrection 9
    Post-Resurrection..9
    Ishmael vs. Isaac..10
    The Symbolism of the Cross 11

Chapter 3: The Crucifixion, Death, and Resurrection of Jesus Christ 14
    Prophecies: Messiah and the Crucifixion..14
    History Recorded by Secular Historians...17
    New Testament Books, Including the Four Gospels, Twenty-one Letters /Epistles, and Acts ..19
    God and Creeds..20
    Lapse of Time Between Events, Reports, and Recordings?...........................21
    Overall Chronology of Key People, Events, Reports, Writings, and Old and New Testament Letters and Books 23
    Old Testament Blood Sacrifice 28
    Cain and Abel...28
    Abraham and Isaac..29
    Key Details of Reported and Recorded Evidence, Events, and Facts Regarding Jesus Christ's Resurrection 31
    The Curse 32
    The Folded Head Cloth 33
    The Two Guards and an Empty Tomb 35
    More Appearances 35
    A Small Miracle 36
    Convert the Enemy /Saul Becomes Paul 37
    The Thorn...38
    The Skeptic and Changed Lives 38
    Study - Not Blind Faith 40
    Committed Doers of Evil..44
    Miracles of Jesus 45
    Shroud of Turin 45

Why did Jesus - Son of God-and God- have to die? 46

Chapter 4: The Ascension of Jesus Christ, the Great Commission, Free Will,
Freedom, and the Return of Jesus Christ...49
Trusting in God 51
Meaning of Life 53
Free Will and Freedom 53
Elimination of Prejudice and Inequality 55
Christian Exclusivity?..55
Answering the Question of Christ's Resurrection 57
The Mere Fact or Event of the Resurrection Itself..59
Now, Where Are YOU Going?..62

PART II. Reason for Our Hope: Undeniable Proof of Our Creator God

I.Faith And Reason 65
II. All of Nature with Its Incredible Magnificence, Provision, Regularity and Order..............67
III. Science...68
IV. The Universe (& More Science) 69
V. Archeological Findings - or Non-findings - Wholly Supporting Scripture........................71
VI. The Truth that Scripture is God's Word - and that God's Word Is True! All Prophecies proven 100%
Accurate. 73
VII. Jesus, the Messiah/Christ: His Birth, Life, Crucifixion and Death............................74
VIII. The Bodily Resurrection of the Messiah - Jesus Christ 75
IX. Jesus Christ - the ONLY person in all of History who declared. 75
X. Why a Messiah- Jesus Christ? - the "Legal" Issue 76
XI. Deposits within each of us of a Free-Will and Creative Mind Possessing a Self consciousness, a
Conscience and Innate Search for Meaning, Purpose, Right & Wrong, Plus a Dream Capacity................76
XII. Evil: Its Origination, Place and End...76
XIII. Total Inability of Any Human to Fully Comply with the Laws of Moses and the Ten Commandments
- Not a Single One of the Abrahamic Faithful nor Those Who Have Been Converted to Christ, despite
Possessing the Indwelling Holy Spirit 77
XIV. Worldwide Institutions of Caring - All Established Only as a Result of Jesus' Teachings of Love, Caring,
Giving, Sacrifice Giving Rise to Christian Discipling and Witness 77
XV. Revolutionary Changes in People Occurring Only as the Result of Their Conversion...........78
XVI. Daily God Experiences/Communications /Dreams /Directions /Strength/Comfort
and Miracles...78
XVII. Thousands of Near-Death Experiences of People - Allowed to Briefly Visit
Christ Before Returning to the World 78
XVIII. With a Sincere and Pure Heart, Ask God in Prayer to Reveal Himself to You! 79
XIX. OK - It is Clear that God Created Us- But Just Who Created God??...........................79
XX1. NOW, and Finally- How about YOU? 79

PART III. Life's Reality Play

I. Content 82
II. Preface 83
III. Observations of Acts And Scenes 85
    A. Observations of the Overall Play 85
    B. Observations of Act I, Scene 1 85
    C. Observations of Act I, Scene 2 86
    D. Observations of Act I, Scene 3 88
    E. Observations of Act I, Scene 4 89
        Warnings against Being "of the World" 91
        The Mission of Christians 91
        Christian Engagement in the World 92
        Voting? 92
        But is Not America - A Christian Nation? 92
        Salt, Light and Salvation Is Messiah Christ's Plan 93
        The Twin Supports 93
    F. Observations of Act I, Scene 5 93
    G. Observations of Act II 95
    H. Observations of Act 111 96
IV. God's Play Lasts Thousands of Years - Why So Long? 97
V. God Is A Loving God! 98
VI. God Hates Evil 98
VII. Why Does God Allow Any Evil In Act I - Even If The Good Outweigh All The Bad ? Why Did God Create Lucifer In The First Place? 100
VIII. Some Insights Into God's Conversion Process 105
IX. The Nations of Israel And America 107
X. Final Notes 109
    What Triggered This Little Book? 109
    By The Way, Just Who Is The Audience In God's Reality Play? 110
About the Author 111
Index 113

Dedication

First and foremost, this book is dedicated to the service of our Lord and Savior, Jesus Christ.

We also dedicate this book:

To the many victims of prejudice and inequality in this World, past and present, and the unsaved souls in our families and the world.

To Peggy, deceased but alive with the Lord, beloved wife of Roger and mother of Matthew, sister of Tammy, whose wrongful death case in California required much travel, capturing critical blocks of time to work on this book.

To Nancy, my devoted wife and partner for sixty-two years, and prime manuscript man ager for this republished book.

To our four faithful children Mark, Christian, Jennifer and Stephen, who have delighted us by seeing each of them become better lawyers (one a judge) and parents than I ever was, adding to our family their wonderful life-mates, Lori, Peter, Gene and Amy, and giving us nine precious grandchildren, Joshua Mark, Luke Joseph, Lea Marie, Gabriella Nicole, Alexia Grace, Jacob Sebastian, Kiera Jane, Bridie Kathleen, and Matthew John.

To sister Dodie, brother Richard, brother-in-law Charles, and all of our families' parents and grandparents, including, in particular, Mary, Kathy, Juanita, Marjorie, Pearl, Richard, Charles, Sebastian, and Joe.

To Will Franklin, my grandfather and great grandson (times six) of John Franklin (brother of the Ben Franklin), who raised thirteen children with his great, discipling wife, Naomi, who read to the family daily from the Bible (the only book the family owned) in the Great Smoky Mountains at Crossnore, North Carolina. Will was ahead of his time in being distrustful of "public education," and he was upset when his firstborn, McCoy, became the first of many to leave home upon reaching 21 out of a desire to get a formal education. McCoy went on to become an ordained minister and a highly sought speaker and preacher followed by several other family members going into Christian ministry. Despite Will's total lack of formal education, he built, largely with his own plans and hands, several buildings in his community. At age sixty-five, to honor McCoy's return to Crossnore to pastor the church, Will built the incredibly beautiful stone and timber Presbyterian Church of Crossnore, a building now designated as a National Historic Landmark (see photo).

To Martin Luther, an alleged great-grandfather (times nine) of our family through Luther's maternal grandmother, M. Zeigler of Eisleben, Germany, and Zurich, Switzerland, whose descendent Barbara Zeigler married into the Otto side of our family in 1850 and came to reside in Harmony, Pennsylvania.

Finally, to Bonnie Gift, now with our Lord, my loyal administrative assistant, for her many years of dedicated service and her many hours helping to prepare the original manuscript for this book; second to Rose Rodriguez, who greatly encouraged this new book's publication

Acknowledgements

We would like to acknowledge Reverend Dennett H. Buettner, Rector of Church of the Savior (COTS) in Ambridge, Pennsylvania, former lawyer and counselor, whose only client is now the chief counselor and advocate for all of us—Jesus Christ—and who gave special attention to our early manuscript.

We also wish to acknowledge:

- Bishop Right Reverend Dr. John Rodgers, Retired Bishop, AMIA, and Dr. Peter Moore, both former Dean/Presidents Emeritus of Trinity School for Ministry, Ambridge, PA;

- Bishop Right Reverend Dr. J. Mark Zimmerman, Bishop of the Anglican Church in North America, Southwest Diocese, Albuquerque, New Mexico, former Rector of Somerset Anglican Fellowship, and St. Francis in the Fields Episcopal Church, Somerset, PA;

- Reverend John Guest, Rector/Senior Pastor of Christ Church at Grove Farm, Sewickley, former Rector of St. Stephens Church, Sewickley, PA and Founding Evangelist of JGET, whose Gospel message has brought many souls to Christ.

- Reverend Geoff Chapman and Reverend Clint Kerley of St. Stephen's Church, Sewickley, Pennsylvania, Reverend Steve Palmer, currently Associate Pastor under Senior Pastor, Rev. Eric Taylor at St. Philips Church, Moon Township, PA;

- Reverend Don Judy, Pastor, Laurel Mountain Chapel, Rockwood, PA; and Reverend John Corbett, Rector, Somerset Anglican Fellowship, Somerset, PA.

- To the many other ministers of God's Word and Truth who influenced me over the years, including E. Jerome Alexis, Chaplain Bob Ford, Steve Smith, Mike Henning, and Bill Henry.

One will not find more genuine, faithful ministers of the Gospel and witnesses to the Lord, dedicated to the Great Commission of our Lord Jesus Christ.

Finally, I acknowledge my wife, Nancy, God's greatest gift and life's helpmate, who is our resident watercolor artist. Her simple, impressionistic interpretations of Scripture illustrated in this book alone warrant attention. My wife and partner of sixty-two years devoted herself to our marriage, raising our four children and later managing a small Christian bookstore. She gave up her prolific artistry twenty-five years ago—much to the chagrin of family—and was urged by family and several dear friends to re-ignite her talent. Wouldn't you know God used this little book endeavor to inspire her return to honoring God through illustrating more of His story and marvelous creation!

We publish this new book with the same objectives as previously, to help you and your children to:

- know your Creator God, His one and only Son, the Messiah Christ, and the Holy Spirit Comforter;

- know God's Love and Blessings, but also His Holiness and Justness;

- secure Eternal Life, a life without Evil and with Indescribable Joy;

- give your current life in this world its true meaning and purpose;

- give you a love for and fear of God that will cast out riff other fears;
- give you a love for all others;
- and finally, give you a peace which passeth all human understanding.

Forward

- LIFE'S TWO QUESTIONS
- PROTECT YOUR CHILDREN
- THE ISIS CRISIS & THE COVID-19 PANDEMIC
- FREE WILL & FREEDOM
- MEANING OF LIFE
- PREJUDICE AND INEQUALITY
- CHRISTIAN EXCLUSIVITY
- CHRISTIAN CHRONOLOGY
- GOSPEL FACTS

A quick glance at the Table of Contents and Index of this small book will reflect the Author's presentation of a volume of cogent facts, evidence and references from both inside and outside of Scripture bearing on whether the Resurrection of Jesus is fact or fiction.

And, if fact, the author describes what this means for each one of us.

If resurrected, this is easily THE central event in all of History - past, present or future. Why? Quite simply, it is the difference for each and every one of us as to whether our earthly life –

- will have been but a "vanishing mist";

   or

- will be a mere passage-way — much like passing through a foreign country before returning to our native country, in this case Eternity!

And, by the way, this life eternal will be with a real and perfect body and doing things which you like and are able to do! Recall just one day of this short life that was really special. — now imagine all days far better and for eternity!

Should we choose to not believe that Jesus was resurrected - read on — because fact is fact, truth is truth and non-belief erases neither.

Whether seeker, agnostic, atheist, skeptic, religious, non-religious, young or old — this book will present facts and evidence you may have never considered or even heard about.

Whether it be the warning of 9/11, covid-19, or far more severe other events to come, we all know that we face increasing dangers, not just somewhere else, but right here in River City, USA; dangers never before experienced, originating from both within and without. Sadly, it is our young people and our precious children and grandchildren that are at greatest risk.

Do you really think any of us can provide assured protection and safety to our children (or ourselves) through education, instruction, warnings, guns, police or armies or the eternal effort of trying to persuade peoples and nations to behave whatever that means? No, not on your life nor theirs! In fact, there is but one and only way to 100% assured and guaranteed safety, life and to discover the meaning of life, not just for now, but forever! It is the way announced to the World 1,985 years ago by a 33-year-old Jewish man he said:

"I am the Way, the Truth, and the Life. No one comes to the Father except through me."

Finally, we have republished this book including many additional facts to the Resurrection and adding two (2) new parts.

I. RESURRECTION: FACT OR FICTION?
A TRIAL LAWYER LOOKS AT ALL
OF THE EVIDENCE

II. REASON FOR OUR HOPE —
Undeniable Proof of Our Creator God

III. LIFE'S REALITY PLAY

ACT I: LIFE IN THIS WORLD
ACT II: A NEW WORLD KING
ACT III: PURELY ELECTIVE

PART I

Resurrection: Fact or Fiction

A Trial Lawyer Looks at All of the Evidence

"Resurrection: Fact or fiction, is an interesting and compelling blend of logic, debate, and historical information from both scriptural and secular sources. Shining through it all is a genuine concern for the spiritual state of every individual as if relates to the resurrection of Jesus Christ."

Editor

Wilbur McCoy (Joe) Otto

1

World Crises

Ishmael v. Isaac

Virtually every generation has faced war, or the tragic effects of conflict and war, and has suffered many lives lost—most often, young lives. Although we have heard this many times before, it's like the little boy who cried wolf too often, and there is great risk that we will ignore or dis- count warnings of future wars. Nevertheless, biblical prophecy, which is 100 percent correct to date, predicts with great specificity a further series of crises in the Middle East, all leading up to a final battle that will bring about the destruction of much that we know today.

Whether that battle will be waged against terrorists, extremists, or groups going by another name, it is clear that the current battle lines were ordained long ago between the offspring of the two sons of Abraham: Ishmael and Isaac. While it is likely that the final battle phase will employ nuclear weaponry, which will cause some degree of fire as a means of destruction, all biblical predictions and references indicate that God Himself will provide most of the fire,[1] just as He provided the water for Noah's world-wide flood.[2] Who among us can possibly look at the history of the world and current world events and not see the coming of major crises?

More than 1,000 Bible prophecies have been proven 100 percent correct to date, and there is no chance that the following six key predictions/promises/clear inferences-all referenced in Scripture-will fail to materialize:

1. While Scripture is less than specific, most agree that Revelation offers no basis to believe that America will have any principal role in the final great battle. While we all witness America's decline from its former dominant position on the international stage, it is submitted that the fundamental reason for the absence of any major role for America once the seven-year tribulation period is about to commence, will be attributable to the rapture of the church and the vast impact this will have on America's population, strength, power, and vitality at the critical hour. Prior to the tribulation America's primary vulnerability will be the potential destruction, or incapacitation of our nation's military and industrial complexes by means of a hostile attack on our electronic/electric infrastructure, a strategy that is undoubtedly being planned at this moment.

---

1.   "By the same word the present heavens and earth are reserved for fire, being kept for the day of judgment and destruction of ungodly men" (2 Peter 3:5-7).

2.   God promised Noah that He would never again destroy mankind by flood, creating the rainbow (which is not the result of evolution) as the sign of His covenant and promise. (See Genesis 9:11-17.) However, in Revelation, John was told of the last battle in the tribulation period that would result in the death of "a third of mankind [not by water but] by the three plagues of fire, smoke and sulfur" this after previous destruction of one-fourth of all mankind for a total loss of one half of the world population. (See Revelation 9:15-18 and 6:7-8)

2. As is almost always the case, the Middle East, and Israel in particular, will hold center stage in the final crises. Israel will have been deceptively promised protection and will be in a relatively vulnerable mode when it is initially attacked.[3]

3. The reestablishment of Israel's new homeland in 1948 was clearly foretold in Isaiah 43, Jeremiah 30, and Ezekiel 56-37 Some even contend that the precise year, 1948, can be projected from Daniel. It is clear that God has promised that the re-emerged, extant nation of Israel will never be destroyed, though it will ultimately require God's miraculous rescue through fire, earthquake, and water to save it (Zech.I4).[4]

4. The forces against Israel will come from among its close neighbors, but they will also include foes from many nations beyond the Middle East, including west, north, and east. (Ezek. 38-39)

5. One third of the world's remaining population after the rapture of the church will suffer death from fire, plagues, and various environmental forces (Rev. 9:15-18).

6. Finally, we are to take comfort in knowing that the faithful will be the ultimate victors under God's reign!

7. We should also take note of two of the great underlying themes of the Old Testament: namely, God's commands to all peoples and nations (1) to give thanks to God for all good things, as these come only from Him and not from themselves and (2) to honor and respect Israel (God's chosen people through whom He has revealed Himself to all mankind), which is particularly relevant here. These two commands come with a corollary promise by God to bless those who bless, and to curse those who curse Israel (Gen. 12:3).

We should also take note of two of the great underlying themes of the Old Testament: namely, God's commands to all peoples and nations (1) to give thanks to God for all good things, as these come only from Him and not from themselves and (2) to honor and respect Israel (God's chosen people through whom He has revealed Himself to all mankind), which is particularly relevant here. These two commands come with a corollary promise by God to bless those who bless, and to curse those who curse Israel (Gen. 12:3).

---

3. The surest sign of the closeness of the final crisis will be when we observe that Israel has rebuilt its third temple in Jerusalem and has entered into or has been granted a seven-year period of promised peace or "protection."

4. It is difficult for many to understand but vie must all keep in mind that "our struggle is not against flesh and blood but against the rulers, against the authorities, against the spiritual forces of evil in the heavenly realms" (Eph. 6:12)

Warning of 9/11

We all remember 9/11! This was no mere isolated, evil event. While certainly not an act desired by God, God allowed this evil attack to serve as a warning to America to not abandon Israel, and for America to turn (or return) to Him—not ourselves—for our Nation's guidance and protection.[5]

George Washington at our Nation's founding in his first inaugural address on April 30, 1789, dedicated America's guidance, and protection to God'ssovereignty.[6] Unknown to many, this address was delivered in NY. City — then the Nation's Capital. However, not just N.Y. city, but this inaugural address was given in St. Paul's Chapel then and now still standing at the corner of Ground Zero!

St. Paul's stone structure was miraculously protected by a large Sycamore tree situated between the Church and the North Tower. The tree, however, was felled!

Note well that America's leadership did not accept the 9/11 warning, and instead responded with, "WE [the U.S.] will re-build" — some even adding "we are defiant!' Would you believe that it is at Isaiah 9:10 and 9:11 that scripture references Israel's response to the Assyrians attack 2,500 years ago as well as foretelling America's response in 2001? On 9/12/01, the U.S. Senate Majority Leader speaking on Capital Hill quoted this scripture by stating -

> "... the bricks have fallen down, but WE will rebuild with dressed stone; the fig [sycamore] trees have been felled but WE will replace them with cedars." [IS. 9:10]

And the Senator then added:

> "That is what WE will do. WE will rebuild and WE will recover.'

At Ground Zero, America has not only constructed the new "Freedom" Tower higher than the Twin Towers, but also in Battery Park adjoining Ground Zero, America has:

- laid 20 tons of hewn granite from the Adirondacks, as a symbol of "America's strength"; and has

- replaced the stricken Sycamore tree with a large Evergreen tree [a member of the Cedar family] naming it the "Tree of Hope."

---

5.   Note: In the 1960's and over subsequent years, the Supreme Court has banned in America's schoolrooms:
- Prayer;
- Bible reading;
- the Ten Commandments; and
- "one Nation under God" in the flag pledge.

    Also, since the 1960's observe the growing proliferation in the US of:
- materialism and pluralism;
- pornography and sexual activity;
- self-worship; idol worship; and
- abortions.

6.   See Deuteronomy 30:16-1

As such, both Israel 2,500 years ago, and America after 9/11/01 gave the Is. 9:10 response, ignoring the warning and adopting a prideful attitude, thereby incurring God's wrathful judgment as set forth in the succeeding verse at IS. 9:11:

"... but the Lord has strengthened ... [Israel's] foes against them and has spurred their enemies on."

Note well that in addition to the physical attack on 9/11, severe financial losses also occurred in America as a result. You may not know that the N.Y. Stock Exchange also stands adjacent to Ground Zero, and it was built on the site of Federal Hall where the first U.S. Congress met.

Further, just outside is a statue of none other than George Washington, and unlike the impact on the stock market, the statue was unharmed by the attack.

In this connection, careful note should be taken of the Old Testament scriptural references to God's blessings, removal of financial debt and acts of judgment rendered at seven-year intervals.[7] (See Lev. 25 re: Sabbath years.)

Thus, almost to the day in September 2008, seven years after 9/11/01, the nation's worst stock market/financial decline occurred with a loss of 777 points! America will do well to take notice and give appropriate response to events yet to occur in this 2015 year, the next seven-year cycle.[8]

Covid-19 Pandemic

As we write this new book the Covid-19 pandemic has replaced 9-11 as God's most recent "Attention Getter," relative to its triggering events, its initial effects, and its eventual results including economic impact. God knows that without both personal and economic loss there is no spiritual gain. God's love for his children is endless, as such God disciplines us in the hope that His temporary discipline will prevent our permanent death. You say how could a loving God cause such pain — I say, how could He not! Spare the rod and spoil the child may not be "politically correct" in this present day of rampant sin, but be assured it is a Godly edict, when done in love.

While 9-11 had its God centered results, they were short-lived, and the overall state of both America and the world has — as the result of God's gift of free-will and the work of counsel — Satan has only grown worse. One singular proof of this is the extreme and almost universal fear and anxiety caused by Covid-19 compared to the fear in America of 9/11 or any of its predecessor events.

---

7. Note: Our Federal bankruptcy laws offer relief of the effects of one's indebtedness after 7 years.
8. Also see "The Harbinger" by Jonathan Cahn, published by Frontline Charisma Media, 2011

For a moment, compare the worldwide Covid-19 deaths occurring in the first half of 2020 with the small handful of events and resulting deaths set forth following:

- the Great Flood (death of all people disobedient to Cod in the entire world);
- the Plagues of Egypt (an untold number);
- the Crusades (1-3 million);
- the Bubonic or Black Plague (25 million — or 1/3 of all Europe!);
- the Revolutionary War (37,000);
- the Civil War (700,000);
- WW I (16 million worldwide);
- Influenza Epidemic in 1918-19 (1.5 million in America, over 50 million worldwide);
- Chinese Civil War (8-12 million);
- Pearl Harbor attack (2,400) and WW II (50 million worldwide)
- 9-11 attack on World Trade Center (3,500).

As to the clear evidence of an ever-increasing unholy and disobedient people — all headed for permanent death absence one's acceptance of God's Plan of Salvation — observe the following:

- *The world's fear of anything — and everything — other than Holy God when he teachers us to:*
  "Fear not, for I am with you…" (Isaiah 41:10)
  "Even though I walk through the valley of the shadow of death, I will fear no evil for you are with me…"
  (Ps 23.4)
  "…me will not ear; though the earth be moved, and though the mountains be carried into the midst of the sea…" (Ps. 46.2)
- Breakdown of the Sanctity of Marriage and traditional family educational units (currently over half of all "families" lack either traditional/marriage — or any
- Love of oneself, rather than God;
- Desire for self-control rather than God-control;
- Deference to man's knowledge, "science,' and progressive "education" rather than God's knowledge and wisdom;
- Love for and dependence on money and self-control;
- Disobedience of virtually all of God's Ten Commandments, including the duty of all to preserve life;
- Church vacancies;
- Idol worship including politics, political correctness, money, power, sports, etc.;
- Seeking of central government and/or world rule rather than God (recall Babel?);
- Drugs and 24/7 pervasive sexual depravity (recall Babylon?);
- Seeking one's "heaven," here on earth — rather than in God's Heaven;
- Simple belief in "a god" rather than loving and trusting in the one Creator and Holy God;
- Creating a god in our image, rather than obedience to the God who made us in HIS image.
- "Abandoning" our children to "tenured" college professors, 95% of whom are adherents to far left socialism, many under influence of Chinese communism who teach capitalist shortcomings and Marxist strengths. [witness current rioting, etc.]

Are Your Children and Grandchildren Safe?

While I was in Southern California recently, I saw a large poster that said, "Parents, in the event of a disaster or emergency, do you know where your children are so you will be able to get them and bring them to safety?"

Attachment to our children is perhaps the strongest emotional connection we have, though it should be exceeded by our attachments first to God and second to spouse. Even as it is God's wish that "none should perish," and as He assures us that none of His sheep will perish, so too it is a strong instinct in each of our hearts to keep our children safe and to do all we can to "save" them. If only we could. [9]Indeed, it is this supreme desire to see our children and grandchildren protected and "saved" that motivated me to write this book.

No one will be saved by us. Ultimate protection and salvation are available to all through Jesus Christ. No matter how diligent and watchful we are, no matter what electronic devices we may employ, ultimately, we ourselves can offer no final protection— and certainly not salvation—to our children. Certain and eternal salvation can come only from God. What a relief it is to know that this is an absolutely sure way to provide certain protection and salvation to our children, particularly in this world filled with danger arid the certainty of great suffering in the years ahead.

Let us recall God's reminder that man's life, compared to life eternal, is but a mere mist that soon vanishes. Who among us would wish to trade an eternity for this mist? And yet most of us are doing just that.[10]

The Two Most Important Questions in Every Human's Life

Since AD 30,[11] virtually every human being has faced two important questions that he must answer before his life here on earth ends.[12]

- Was Jesus, in fact, resurrected?
- If Jesus was in fact resurrected—a fact independent of whether or not we believe it— what does that mean to me and my soul, not just here on earth but for eternity?

The first and most important question is not whether anyone in the history of the world has ever been resurrected but rather whether Jesus was resurrected after His crucifixion death.

Accordingly, there is not a scintilla of evidence in world history to suggest that anyone other than Jesus was ever resurrected, including Buddha, Confucius, Muhammad, Joseph Smith, or anyone else.[13]

These two questions—and mankind's quest to answer them—are not an elective. They are mandatory. Thus, if we choose not to take the "exam," or we ignore it or delay taking it, we receive a failing grade. There will be no "incompletes," no second chances, and no reincarnations.

---

9. For me, and perhaps for you, the single most painful event in life is to see a child suffer from pain caused by an adult. Our Father God has surely created within each of us the same feelings and emotions that He Himself holds for His children.

10. What is your life? You are a mist that appears for a little while and then vanishes" (James 4:14).

11. All dates cited throughout are approximate, and scholars will differ within a range of a few years.

12. "Those who died prior to AD 30 or without knowledge of Jesus will be judged by God according to the Abrahamic covenant; their response to the revelation of God through nature, God's creation, and creative order; and the conscience placed within each of us—or otherwise, as God's mercy determines (Rom. 1:18-23; 2:1-16; Ex. 33:19).

13. Note that Lazarus, the Roman soldier's son, and the poor woman's son, among other cases, are reported in Scripture to have been raised by Jesus from death. These were temporary "resuscitations" only.

The Centrality of the Issue of the Resurrection of Jesus Christ

Jesus Christ's assurance of ultimate protection and salvation—and the promise of a resurrected body for eternity—for each of His children is wholly dependent on the central issue in all of history, which is also the central issue of Christianity: namely, the resurrection of Jesus Christ. Is Christ's resurrection fact or fiction?

Paul clearly expressed the central and pivotal issue of the entire gospel and Christianity as follows: "And if Christ has not been raised, our preaching is useless, and so is your faith. More than that, we are then bound to be false witnesses about God ... If the dead are not raised, then Christ has not been raised either. And if Christ has not been raised, your [our] faith is futile; you [we] are still in your [our] sins. If only for this life we have hope in Christ, we are to be pitied more than all men" (I Cor. 15:14-19)

2

Key World Facts, Circumstances, and Status

Calendar Dating

This book is being written in the year AD 2020. (Anno Domini, or AD, means "in the year of our Lord.") This is 2024 years after the year of Jesus' birth in 4 BC. (All years before year one has been marked as BC, meaning "before Christ") I submit that if Jesus Christ had not been resurrected after His crucifixion death—an event that quickly became known and accepted world- wide—the world's dating system would not have pivoted around Jesus Christ's birth!

Christianity

Pre-Resurrection

Jesus Christ was born in 4 BC and was crucified in AD 30. While few people dispute the claim that Jesus Christ was crucified, some question whether Jesus actually died, despite the lack of evidence that a wounded, barely alive Jesus was walking around after crucifixion.[1]

Jesus Christ's ministry began in AD 27 and extended for three and a half years. During this time, Jesus Christ chose twelve apostles to work with Him, and there were thousands who knew that Jesus Christ was someone special and maybe even the Messiah. Still, there were no "Christian" churches, temples, synagogues, meeting places, or places of worship established prior to Jesus' resurrection.

Post-Resurrection

Following Jesus Christ's resurrection — or widely reported resurrection — Peter worked primarily among the Jews, and Paul worked among the Gentiles. During the thirty-four-year period between AD 30 and AD 64, they and their followers were spreading the gospel, which was centered on the fact of Jesus Christ's resurrection. Persecutions of Christians commenced immediately, resulting in taking the lives of all of Jesus' apostles, including Paul, and excepting only John. Jesus' apostles, including Paul, and excepting only John. This prosecution continued throughout the Mideast for 300 years (recall Christians being fed to the lions in the Roman Coliseum under Nero and others.) despite which Christianity not only survived — it exploded. Christian churches were rapidly formed and spread throughout the Mideast and surrounding regions.

---

1. Muslims contend Jesus was whisked directly from life to Heaven and deny that God could suffer for mortal man.

"Churches' were often groups of Believers meeting in homes —i.e., home groups.

By AD 327, this included what is now Italy, Greece, Turkey, Germany, Britain, Lebanon, Iran, Israel, Syria, Egypt, Sudan, Ethiopia, and Armenia. Between AD 64 and AD 325, no other religion grew so fast or so far — and by *peaceful* means, unlike some others. In this regard, the heart of Christianity was a message of peace and love that was never intended to be a "religion." Rather, it was meant to be a unique relationship between each individual and Jesus Christ, who was one of a kind, a God-man who was fully God.

The Council of Nicea in 325 AD under King Constantine canonized all twenty-seven books of the New Testament. By then, Constantine was not dictating a new religion; he was merely authenticating what was already the most accepted religion throughout the entire Mediterranean region. In AD 380 Christianity was declared to be the official state religion of the entire Roman Empire under Emperor Theodosius. Imagine it: this was just Who years after the Romans had allowed Jesus to be crucified!

Pause here for a moment, and recognize that while Jesus, as the Jewish Messiah, did not conquer Caesar and the Romans militarily as the Jews had anticipated, in a very real sense and even more effective and meaningful manner -

- the Word has replaced the Sword; and
- Jesus conquered all Caesars in the world arena!

Christianity has spread rapidly, not by violence but through peaceful sharing of the Word by Christ's disciples throughout the world. Currently, Christianity is the fastest-growing religion within China, Korea, Africa and Indonesia.

Ishmael vs. Isaac

Note the stark difference between Christianity and other religious groups. Tradition holds that, except for John, all of Jesus's apostles, gospel authors, and closest disciples willingly gave their lives for Jesus, for they knew personally that He had been crucified and then resurrected.[2] Jesus, the founder of Christianity, died sacrificially and was resurrected, and He promised future resurrected, eternal bodies to all who would follow Him.

Contrast Christianity with any religion or group whose leader or founder did not die for his followers, was *not* resurrected, and did *not* promise resurrection to others. Rather, these other leaders have asked their followers to die for their religion or to kill those who refuse to follow or convert to their ways—with or without the promise of later reward. Take note of the origins and prophesied destinies of the descendants of Isaac as opposed to the descendants of Ishmael.

On His spiritual side, Jesus was the Son of God. On His human side, being born of the Virgin Mary, Jesus was a descendant in the line of Isaac (born in 2066 BC), the son of Abraham and his wife, Sarah. God covenanted and promised that this bloodline would produce the Savior of the world

---

2. Paul was beheaded in Rome under Nero. Andrew was crucified in Greece. Peter was crucified (upside down) in Rome. Thomas was speared in India. Luke was crucified in Athens. Simon (the Zealot) was crucified in Britain. Mark was dragged through the streets of Alexandria. Bartholomew was crucified and beheaded in Armenia. James Alphaeus and James, brother of Jesus, were stoned in Jerusalem. James, son of Zebedee, the first Apostle to be martyred, was killed by the sword in Jerusalem. Phillip was crucified in Hierapolis. Jude Joe crucified in Mesopotamia. Matthias was stoned and beheaded in Jerusalem. Judas, the traitor, died by his own hand. Matthew was beheaded in Ethiopia

Ishmael was born in 2080 BC, the illegitimate son of Abraham and his servant Hagar. From him descended Muhammed,[3] born in AD 570, who produced the Qur'an (purported to have been dictated by the angel Gabriel). God prophesied of Ishmael: "A wild donkey of a man, his hand will be against everyone, and everyone against him and he will live in hostility toward all his brothers" (Gen. 16:12). "I will make him fruitful and will greatly increase his numbers. He will be the father of twelve rulers, and I will make him into a great Nation" (Gen. I7:20-21).

Further biblical prophecies are being validated and played out on the international scene before our very eyes!

The Symbolism of the Cross

Circa 200 AD, Tertullian, a West African lawyer and theologian, wrote of priests tracing the sign of the cross on the foreheads of confirmants.

Eusebius writes that Emperor Constantine saw a cross of light in the sky and heard the words "conquer by the sign" after his victorious battle of The Milvian Bridge in 312. Thereafter the cross was adopted as the symbol on army standards. (See "Cross of Christ" by John Stott, 1986.)

The symbol of every Christian church — and indeed of Christianity itself — for the past 1500 years has been the cross. One cannot go anywhere in the world without seeing the cross worn or displayed by Christians and many others. I submit that if Christ had died by crucifixion on the cross without being resurrected, the cross would be among the most despicable symbols in the world and would rarely, if ever, be displayed. Certainly, it would not be the central symbol for Christianity — assuming that Christianity would even exist!

The pain of Jesus' crucifixion after His merciless beatings was so great that a new word was first coined in the early years after Jesus' crucifixion — namely "excruciating."

Sunday

Also, despite Saturday having been the Jewish Sabbath for centuries it was only a brief time following Jesus' resurrection (a resurrection celebrated on Sunday despite its likely occurrence after sundown on Saturday that Jewish Christians adopted Sunday for their Sabbath worship.

While the church, for many reasons, has adopted Sunday as resurrection day, there can be no doubt that Jesus was in the tomb for three whole days and three whole nights, which was just as Jesus prophesied when He referenced the story of Jonah and whale (Matt. 12:40). Many argue that a careful reading of the entirety of Scripture supports Jesus having been crucified and dying around 3 p.m. on Wednesday (the "Day of Preparation" before the annual Sabbath and then spending the three full nights of Wednesday, Thursday, and Friday and the three full days of Thursday (the high day Sabbath and the first day of the Feast of Unleavened Bread), Friday and Saturday in the tomb before rising at sunset on Saturday evening. Mark 16:19 States, "Now having risen, early the first day of the week He appeared first to Mary Magdalene." While the Greek has no punctuation, many interpreters have incorrectly placed a comma after "week" instead of "risen," which would tend to (incorrectly) support a Sunday morning resurrection.

---

3. It is reported that Muhammad believed much of the Bible to be essentially accurate and uncorrupted, including the fact that Jesus was born of a virgin and ascended to heaven (though not crucified and resurrected)

Therefore, when the women came to the tomb on Sunday morning, the guards were long gone, the stone had been rolled away, the tomb was empty, Jesus was not there (having risen at sunset on Saturday), and the angel(s) said, "Why do you look for the living among dead? He is not here, he has risen." (Matt.28).

Likewise, not long after the resurrection, Christians began to celebrate both baptism and communion rituals. Baptism represents rebirth, and the communion ritual memorializes Jesus's sacrificial death. Can you imagine this happening if Jesus had not been resurrected after His death? Does anyone celebrate the deaths of Moses, Muhammad, George Washington, or Abe Lincoln?

Of course, we must note very carefully that there is one person whose death we do celebrate. Jesus commanded us to celebrate His death. This is simply because His resurrection would have no meaning to us if we did not first accept the fact of His death and understand His personal sacrifice for each of us!

Naming customs are attributable to a resurrected, not dead, Jesus. To illustrate the point, consider the names of our children and grandchildren: Mark, Stephen, Christians, Joshua, Luke, Matthew, Jacob, Gabriella, Leah, and so on. Such names as Peter, Paul, David, John, Thomas, Joseph, and Mary abound in the world. However, we don't tend to name our children Pontius Pilate, Judas, Caesar, Saul, Nero, Herod, and so on (though we may give our animals these names).

In summary, it is only the resurrection of Christ that gives meaning to the cross, the Christian church, Sunday worship, baptism and communion rituals, and the names of our loved ones — and, frankly, hope, life eternal, faith, love, freedom, and so on.

3

The Crucifixion, Death, and Resurrection of Jesus Christ

The crucifixion and resurrection of Jesus Christ were fully and thoroughly passed on, reported, and recorded as contemporaneous events in notes, writings, records, and by word of mouth. Primarily, they took these forms:

- Prophecies, histories recorded by secular historians
- Early memorized stories, teachings, creeds and hymns
- Sets of notes, memoranda, documents referenced as "Q" (Quelle) Source
- New Testament letters, including the four Gospels

Prophecies: Messiah and the Crucifixion

Of the hundreds of prophecies in the Scriptures all proven true to date, the single greatest are the specific prophecies of the coming of the Messiah, and the Messiah's crucifixion made hundreds of years before the events when God would ordain the sacrifice of His one and only Beloved Son, Jesus Christ, as the only means of consecration and redemption for the sins, of each of us and all mankind.

Danie19:20-27, (Gabriel to Daniel):

Seventy-sevens are decreed for your people and your holy city Io finish transgressions, to put an end to sin, to atone for wickedness, to bring everlasting righteousness, to seal up vision and prophecy, and to anoint the most Holy (Messiah).

Know and understand this. from the issuing of the decree to restore and rebuild Jerusalem (2nd temple 516 BC) until the Anointed One, the ruler (Messiah in 4 BC) comes there will be seven sevens and sixty-two 'sevens.' It will be rebuilt with streets rind a trench, but in times of trouble. After the sixty-two sevens, the anointed one (Messiah) will be cut off (crucifixion in 30 AD) end will have nothing. The people of the ruler (Titus will come and will destroy the city rind the sanctuary (in 70 AD). The (ultimate) end will come like a flood, water will continue until the end, and desolations have been decreed. He (Anti-Christ) will confirm a covenant with many or one seven. In the middle of the seven (3 1⁄2 years) he will put an end to sacrifice and offering ...he will set up an abomination that causes desolation until the end (minor end times) taint is decreed is poured out on him."

This crucifixion event was prophesied with thorough and totally accurate detail - only possible with the inspiration of an all-knowing God[1]

---

1. Do you know anyone who can predict with precision even 3 of 3 specific events? The Bible contains thousands of prophecies by some 66 (57 in OT and 9 in NT) prophets and prophetesses. The great bulk of these have already come to pass, and the record is 100 percent accurate. Peter Stoner, a mathematics professor in Science Speaks, does a mathematical analysis of the chances of just eight

The initial prophetic facts were set forth by Moses when he wrote:

"And you (Satan) *will strike his heel...he (Jesus) will crush your head"* (Gen. 3:15).

This was followed by the incredible story of Abraham and Isaac described later in this chapter. Later still, some 1,030 years before Jesus Christ's crucifixion, David's Psalm 22 contains the descriptions set out following. (The words within brackets that follow the words of the prophecies are either Jesus Christ's own words while hanging on the cross, or they are reported facts and statements of eyewitnesses to the crucifixion.)

"My God, my God, why have you forsaken me?" (Ps. 22:1)
[*"My God, my God, why have you forsaken me?"* (Matt. 87 46).]

*"But I am a worm...scorned by men and despised by the people. All who see me,
they hurl insults"* (Ps. 22:6-7). [*The people mocked Jesus on the cross* (Matt. 27:39)]

"He trusts in the Lord, let the Lord rescue him" (Ps. 22:8),
[*People watching Jesus Christ on the cross said, "Let us see if Elijah comes
to save him! He saved others, but he can't save himself!"* (Matt. 27:43.)]

"I am poured out like water, and all my bones are out of joint" (PS.22:14).
[*Water and blood gushed from Jesus' chest when pierced by a sword* (John 19:30).]

---

prophecies made about one man proving to be correct. Stoner illustrates this likelihood as 1 in 1017 (seventeenth power). This is the same as the chance of a blind man correctly selecting a single marked silver dollar from among a collection of silver dollars stacked 2 feet high across the entire state of Texas!

Referenced here are just 8 of the 50 or more prophecies regarding the identity of the coming Messiah He would be born in Bethlehem. He would be preceded by one announcing His coming. He would enter Jerusalem as a king on a donkey. He would be betrayed by friend for thirty pieces of silver. That silver would be used to buy a potter's field. He would-be put-on trial and would refuse to defend Himself. He would be crucified with thieves (D. Limbaugh, Jesus on Trial, 199).

In all 27% (or 8,352 out of 31,124 verses) of the Bible contain predictive material, with a total of 737 prophetic topics. ("See Encyclopedia of Bible Prophecy," J. Barton Payne, NY Harper & Row.)

The fact that water flowed out of Jesus' side when pierced by the Roman soldier's sword proved that Jesus was already dead since this could only happen if the heart's pumping action had previously failed, caused by his severe beating and suffocation.

> *"My tongue sticks to the roof of my mouth"* (Ps. 22:15). *["I thirst" (John 19:38)]*
> *"They have pierced my hands and my feet"* (Ps. 22:16).
> *[Nails were driven through Jesus' hands and feet (John 20:25; Luke 24:39)]*
>
> *"Do not break and of the bones"* (Ex. 13:46).
>
> *"I can count all my bones"* (Ps. 22:17). *["None of Jesus 'bones were
> broken by the Roman soldiers, who would often break the legs
> to speed up death"* (John 19:36)].

"They divide my garments ... and cast lots for my clothing" (Ps. 22:18). [The soldiers divided Jesus's clothes and cast lots for his tunic (Matt. 27:35).]

Read these prophetic statements, written by Isaiah in 701 BC.

- "He was despised, and rejected by men ... He was despised, and we esteemed him not (Isa. 53:3).
- "But he was pierced for our transgressions, he was crushed for our inequities, and by his wounds we are healed" (v.5)
- "And the Lord has laid on him the inequity of us all" (v. 6).
- "He was led like a lamb to the slaughter and as a sheep before her shearers is silent, so he did not open his mouth" (v. 7)
- "For the transgressions of my people he was taken away" (v. 8).
- "He was assigned a grave with the wicked" (v. 9).
- "Yet it was the Lord's will to crush him and cause him to suffer, and ... the Lord makes his life a guilt offering he will see his offspring and prolong his days, and the will of the Lord will prosper in his hand" (v. 10).
- "After the suffering of his soul he will see the light of life . . . by his knowledge, my righteous servant will justify many, and he will bear their inequities" (v. 11).
- "Because he poured out his life unto death and was numbered with the transgressors, for he bore the sin of many, and made intercession for the transgressors" (v.12)[2]

There are also many prophecies regarding the resurrection of Jesus Christ. Isaiah wrote, "On this mountain the Lord...will swallow up death forever" (Isa. 25:6). "In that day...your dead will live; their bodies will rise "(Isa. 26:1). "The earth will give birth to her dead" (Isa. 26:19)

Jesus prophesied His own death and resurrection on many occasions, but His apostles failed to understand until after the resurrection. Jesus said, "Destroy this temple [my body] and I will raise it again in three days" (John 2:19) "As Jonah was three days and three nights in the belly of a large fish, so the Son of Man will be three days and three nights in the heart of the earth" (Matt. 12:40). "The Son of man is going to be betrayed into the hands of men; they will kill him, and on the third day he will be raised to life" (Matt. 17:22 23).

---

2.   Isaiah 53 is one of the complete chapters found among the Dead Sea Scrolls, which date back to 100 125 BC. They were found by a shepherd in a cave in 1947

Much like the resurrection of Jesus, the total accuracy of Bible Prophesy is itself undeniable and clear and convincing evidence beyond any reasonable doubt of the one and only true God. It is much like the man who built a wall 6 feet wide and 3 feet tall. When asked why wider than tall, the man said, "First, because the wall is unlikely to ever fall, but should it ever be overturned it will be even taller than before".[3]

History Recorded by Secular Historians

Flavius Josephus, a Jewish secular historian born in AD 37, made two primary references to Jesus in his *Jewish Antiquities*, written between AD 75 and 95. The first reference (at 18:3:3) says, "At this time there was a wise man called Jesus...his conduct was good, and he was known to be virtuous...Pilate condemned him to be crucified...But those who had become his disciples did not abandon his discipleship. They reported that he had appeared to them three days after his crucifixion and that he was alive. Accordingly, he was perhaps the Messiah...the tribe of the Christians... has not disappeared to this day."

Josephus's second reference (at 20:9:1) says, "Convening the judges of the Sanhedrin, he (Albinus) brought before them the brother of Jesus, who was called the Christ, whose name was James and some others...he delivered them to be stoned."

While most scholars believe the first reference is largely authentic, some believe that it contains some minor Christian interpolations. The second reference is accepted by all.

Most Jews believed and accepted the fact that Jesus's tomb was found empty. See also the book entitled *Toledoth Jesu*, written in AD 500. It states, "Search was made, and he was not found in the grave where he had been buried."

In addition to Scripture, Justin Martyr wrote a book in AD 150 called *Dialogue with Tryphs*. Chapter 108 reported that the Jews were teaching that Jesus's body had been stolen and that the tomb was empty.

Cornelius Tactitus (ca) 100 AD writes in his Annals, history of Roman Emperors: "Christus, from whom the name (Christians) had its origin, suffered the extreme penalty during the reign of Tiberius at the hand of... Pontius Pilatus..." (Annals 15:44).

Pliny the Younger, Roman legate writing to Emperor Trajan noted that "Christians were refusing to reverence Caesar's image, met regularly and sang hymns 'to Christ as if to God'" (Letters 10:96:7).

Suetonius Tranquillus, librarian, referenced Claudius "banishing the Jews from Rome ... Christus being their leader"

---

3.   See "*Bible Prophecy*" by Mark Hitchcock, Tyndale House, 1999.

27 New Testament Books, Including the Four Gospels, Twenty-one Letters/Epistles, and Acts

First, let's look at the four Gospels — Matthew, Mark, Luke and John. The first three of these are referenced as the Synoptic Gospels — meaning that they include roughly the same content, and order of events, and often action-filled, particularly in Mark and Matthew.

John, clearly written a few years later than the first three books, includes a more developed theology, seeking to both strengthen present believers as well as reaching out to non-believers.

Most noteworthy is the fact that there are no significant differences among any of the material facts and events set forth in any of the four books. Further, whatever minor differences or additional facts or events exist in one or other of the books — given their differing authors and perspectives - are not only natural but reassuring and confirming of rather than detracting from authenticity and credibility.

While the four Gospels were all written within ten or so years of each other, it is important to understand the times existing in 30-100 A.D. The culture of that time valued oral accounts as the best evidence. The apostles and their disciples resorted to writing their accounts only to assist their oral presentations and when it became apparent that the Christian movement would outlast their lifetimes. It was therefore necessary to prepare writings while they were still living in order to perpetuate their testimony for future generations.

As it was in the case of the various creeds and hymns, most of the material had been passed along orally, repeatedly but were eventually outlined in writings or notes before the final texts were prepared. Thus, it is safe to say that much, if not most, of the material appearing in the final letters and books of the New Testament began to develop from day one (or should we say day four), being preserved in the minds, creeds and stories which began to be verbalized in the days following the resurrection of Jesus Christ. Also, keep in mind that all of this is occurring in an era when writing and copying documents were done by hand, using rudimentary writing materials, a feat itself nothing short of miraculous.

It is believed that within a short time a common set of brief writings were developed and used by one or more, and with each perhaps adding to the writings as necessary. Such notes or early writings have been referred to as "Quelle" (source) or "Q" documents.

The two closest books in content are Mark and Matthew, with Matthew containing virtually 93% of the events and subjects set forth in Mark, while Luke contains roughly 30% of the Markan content.[4]

We know that Mark, a scribe, was not an apostle or eyewitness of Jesus, and that the bulk of his writings were dictated to him by the apostle Peter, a close companion.

Matthew was a tax collector but like Peter, he was also an apostle and eyewitness to Jesus, so it is

both understandable and confirming that there would be similarity of content between Mark's and Matthew's writings.

---

4. Some critics claim that Mark's Gospel is "corrupted," because the last twelve verses of Mark16 were not included in an earlier version of the book. However, note well that in previous verses Mark noted that the three women (Mary Magdalene, Mary and Salome) had found Jesus' tomb empty. Mark then goes on to report that Jesus had thereafter appeared to Mary Magdalene, to the two men on the road to Emmaus and to the Eleven, and then referenced Jesus' Great Commission and His Ascension. Rach of these additional reports and references would have been conveyed to Mark by Peter as an eyewitness, and each was also likely reported by Matthew and others to Mark.

Luke — like Mark — was neither an apostle nor eyewitness to Jesus; however, Luke became very close to Paul and also to Peter, so each would have served as a source of material for Luke. Luke was a physician, very science and fact based, qualifying as the only "expert witness" to Christ. Individuals having special competence, training and skills serve as special factfinders and provide opinions — based on careful investigation and analysis. Such experts are highly valued, contributing to admissible evidence in courts of law and their fact-determination process. Accordingly, Luke serves as the only "expert" witness testifying to the authenticity of the Gospel message. Luke also authored Acts, likely written while Paul was imprisoned in Rome. Luke's central purpose was to record the history of the early church in his uniquely expert style, starting immediately following the Resurrection, and revolving primarily around the experiences of Peter and Paul.

Luke, likely referring to Peter, Mark, Matthew, James and Paul, writes:

> "Many have undertaken to draw up an account of the things that have been fulfilled among us just as they were handed down to us by those who from the first were eyewitnesses and servants of the Word. Therefore, since I, myself have carefully investigated everything from the beginning, it seemed good also to me to write an orderly account...so that you may know the certainty of the things you have been taught." (Luke 1:1-4)

While written early, the four Gospel books were not likely the initial New Testament books to appear in final form. Jesus knew what He was doing (of course!) when he "visited upon" Saul — post-resurrection - converting and "transforming" him into Paul. Thus, Paul not only wrote (and like all the Gospel writers, always under the influence of the Holy Spirit) 13 of the 19 New Testament epistles and letters. Paul was likely the first to "publish" a New Testament book, and probably the first 4, namely Galatians, I and II Thessalonians, and I Corinthians all close to 50 A.D., with James' letter also appearing in very close proximity.

While all the New Testament books have as their main underlying and central subject and source of their writings the Lord Jesus Christ, perhaps none more than Paul. Paul is not only the most prolific of the writers, and while not an eyewitness to Jesus during His lifetime, Paul was an eyewitness to Jesus after Jesus' Resurrection, when Jesus suddenly appeared on the road to Damascus blinding Paul for three days. Further, and what is often overlooked is that Jesus Christ Himself revealed the Gospel to Paul. Thus, while Peter dictated most of Mark's writings, Jesus Himself revealed to Paul the bulk of Paul's writings. Read Paul's own words at Gal. 1:11,12, 16-19.

See also similar references to "Christians" in Eusebius's Ecclesiastical History and Origen Contra Celsum

God and Creeds

Note the following incredible testimony from the lips of Paul himself. It witnesses to the fact that he had received the gospel and Word of God, not from man but by direct revelation from Jesus.

> *"I want you to know, brother, that the Gospel I preached is not something that man made up. I did not receive it from any man, nor was I taught it; rather, I received it by revelation from Jesus Christ.* You have heard of my previous way of life in Judaism, how intensely I persecuted the Church of God, and tried to destroy it. I was advancing in Judaism beyond many Jews of my own age and was extremely zealous for the traditions of my father. But when God, who sent me apart from the birth and called me, by his grace, was pleased to reveal his Son to me so that I might preach him among the Gentiles, *I did not consult any man, nor did I go up to Jerusalem to see those who were apostles before I was, but I went immediately into Arabia and later returned to Damascus. Then after three*

years, (in Arabia and Damascus) I went up to Jerusalem to get acquainted with Peter and stayed with him fifteen days. I saw...only James, the Lord's brother. I assure you before God that what I am writing you is no lie. (Gal. 2:11-20, emphasis added.)

It is believed that I Corinthians 15:3-8 is the oldest New Testament Scripture to be clearly referenced among common creeds that existed from the time of Jesus Christ's resurrection in AD 30. It was passed along from person to person until it was set forth in Scripture in AD 50 by the apostle Paul: " For what I received, I passed on to you as of first importance that Christ died for our sins...was buried...was raised on the third day and that he appeared to Peter, then to the twelve...After that he appeared to more than five hundred of the brothers at the same time, most of whom are still living...then to James, then to all the Apostle, and last of all he appeared to me also" (1 Cor. 15:3-8, emphases added.)4

A Creed believed to be sung as a very early Christian Hymn likely withing first two years after Jesus's crucifixion.

> "Who being in very nature God... at the name of Jesus every knee should bow in heaven, and earth and under the earth, and every tongue confess that Jesus Christ is Lord, to the Glory of God the Father" (see Phil. 2:6-11)

As to the timing of the appearances of the Gospels, they should be seen less as linear, and more as nearly parallel, all appearing in close proximity with Mark, Matthew and Luke before the 50's and John in the early 60's.

Finally, note well that 3 of the 4 Gospels, and 24 of the 27 New Testament books were written by "eyewitnesses" to Jesus, with 2 of the remaining 3 books being authored by Luke, the expert who relied substantially on eyewitness accounts. This leaves as the sole remaining book, Hebrews, which is believed to have been written by Apollos, an early companion of Paul. Hebrews is a highly analytical summary of Jesus' teachings and Christianity for the primary benefit of the Jews based largely on the eyewitness reports of Peter and Paul.

Lapse of Time Between Events, Reports, and Recordings?

Many people have the impression that the Bible, and in particular the New Testament, records events that occurred many years — decades or even a century or more before the writings. Of course, even if any time lapse would be significant, it would not necessarily impact truth or accuracy. Historically the custom of telling and retelling facts, news, events, and stories especially within a culture that revered truthful reporting would favor accuracy and credibility.

However, as noted in the preceding section any time lapse between the crucifixion/resurrection events and appearance of the creeds, hymns, orations, and the "Q" documents was likely in terms of months not years with New Testament books beginning to appear within 10 to 20 years.

In this further regard note that while stories reporting on the deaths of more recent public figures — such as Lincoln, Kennedy, and King—occurred immediately, writings have continued now for over one hundred years, with later efforts often revealing additional facts and detail.

Of course, in the case of Jesus, the only reason Jesus' crucifixion and death have been reported in such detail, not only immediately but continuously over all time since, is because of Jesus' Resurrection — the most unprecedented, singular, spectacular event of all time — and an event which guaranteed perpetual focus on Jesus' life and being. Further, even the rare attacks on the accuracy or authenticity of the events have only served to reinforce the facts regarding Jesus and Truth!

Add to all the above the overarching guidance and protection of the Holy Spirit over the creation, preservation, and truth of all of Scripture and one will quickly conclude that of all fruitless human efforts, attacking Scripture is surely #1.

Overall Chronology of Key People, Events, Reports, Writings, and Old and New Testament Letters and Books[5].

2800 BC	The great flood, and the rainbow/Stonehenge, UK The Bible Describes the Noah flood as world-wide and there are geo-physical remnants world wide. There is also a new report of an Arc-shaped structure in Turkey currently being excavated.
2700 BC	Discovery of writing
2500—2000 BC	Reports, stories, writings, and creeds leading to Old Testaments books
2166 BC	Abram (Abraham) born
2080 BC	Ishmael born to Abraham and Hagar
2066 BC	Isaac born to Abraham and Sarah
2050 BC	Abraham offers Isaac to God as sacrifice
1750 BC	Babylonian/Hammurabi Code
1526 BC	Moses born
1446 BC	Exodus from Egypt
1456 BC	Ten Commandments authored by God[6]
1446-1406 BC	Moses writes Genesis
1000 BC	Psalm 22 and David
965 BC	Solomon
960 BC	Solomon's Temple
780 BC	Jonah
753 BC	Founding of city of Rome
701 BC	Isaiah 53/Assyrians besiege Jerusalem
600 BC	Jeremiah
587 BC	Babylonian Exile/1st Temple destroyed
563 BC	Buddha born
560 BC	Daniel
551 BC	Confucius born
539 BC	King Cyrus of Persia captures Babylon
516 BC	Second Temple is Rebuilt
500 BC	Zechariah
450 BC	Ezra assembles "Hebrew Scriptures," of which several thousand "copies" exist today
448 BC	Athenian power
350 BC	Codex Sinaiticus found in St. Catherine Monastery, Mt. Sinai, in 1859, which includes most of Old Testament
332 BC	Tyre Destroyed by Alexander the Great[7]

5.   All dates are approximate. Many precise dates are unknown, and scholars differ considerably within a fair range. However, for purposes of this chronology, the order of events is more important than the precision of dates, which is illuminating.

6.   A bookstore in Manchester, VT has engraved in its stone entry, "Nothing is written in stone!" How wrong in so many respects!

7.   The Bible's thousands of prophecies, all proven accurate to date, included the fact that the cities of Tyre and Babylon would be destroyed and would never be rebuilt (Jer 51:26, 62-64). Note that Saddam Hussein once threatened to rebuild Babylon, and Saddam did not fare well. In any event, neither city has been rebuilt to date, and if we ever see Tyre or Babylon rebuilt, we can argue that the Bible is all wrong.

250-200 BC	Septuagint Greek translation of Hebrew Old Testament by seventy to seventy-two Jewish scholars
100-150 BC	Dead Sea Scrolls: Accurate scroll copy of Isaiah and other OT books copied by Essenes found in cave in Khirbet Qumran, Israel, by shepherd
63 BC	Pompey captures Jerusalem
45 BC	Julian Calendar
27 BC	Octavious 1st Roman Emperor
5/4 BC	John the Baptist born to Elizabeth
5/4 BC	Jesus Christ's birth, the pivotal point in history

AD 1	Paul and John born
26-27	Jesus' Baptism by John the Baptist
26-36	Pontius Pilate, procurator of Judea
29	In the temple, Jesus reads from Judea from Isaiah and references the writings regarding the Law of Moses, the Prophets, and the Psalms (Luke 24:44-45)
30	Jesus Christ's crucifixion and observed/reported appearances following His resurrection [some argue the date of resurrection to be 4/3/33]
30-31	Creeds referenced in 1 Corinthians 15:3-8
31	Peter begins ministry and spreading of gospel
32	Stephen martyred with Saul present
32-33	Jesus Christ appears to Saul (Paul) on the road to Damascus, and Paul is converted from killing Christians to becoming one and converting others
34-37	Earliest 'Q" Documents
35-4	Paul meets with Peter and also James in Jerusalem
37	Titus Flavius Josephus born (AD 37—100)
40	James, son of Zebedee, is the first of the apostles to be killed for his faith
47-54	Appearance of the earliest books of the New Testament, including Galatians, Thessalonians, Corinthians, James, Philippians, Mark and Matthew,[8] with Luke, Timothy, Acts and John following between 58 and 64.[9]
49	The Nazareth Decree issued by Emperor Claudius prohibiting the opening of graves
52	Thallus' History (see Africanus below in 221)
62	James, brother of Jesus, dies for the faith that he gained only after Jesus' Resurrection
66	Paul is beheaded (under Nero)
67	Peter is crucified, upside down
68	Nero commits suicide
70	Romans, under Titus, destroy the second Jewish temple and virtually all of Jerusalem (FN 11) and the Jews were dispersed from their homeland for the next 1,878 years
80	Pliny the Younger (61-112) wrote to Emperor Trojan: "How are we to deal with these troublesome Christians who meet on a fixed day, sing hymns, etc.?
82	Antiquities of the Jews authored by Titus Flavius Josephus (37-100 AD)
90	Council of Jamnia confirms the Old Testament canon
90-93	Each of the four individual Gospels — are now in wide circulation
100	John dies
110	Cornelius Tacitus in his writings re: Nero references "Christus"
112	Pliny the Younger writes to Emperor Trajan: "I would ask them whether they
130	Papias Historian who speaks of Jesus and His Resurrection
150	A book containing all of Paul's letters, except Titus and Timothy, is in circulation

---

8. Simon Greenleaf, *The Testimony of the Evangelists, 29*, argues for Matthew as earliest.

9. A good argument can be made that since none of the four Gospels reference the huge event in AD 70 of the Roman destruction of the second Jewi8h temple in AD 7, all four Gospels were almost assuredly written before AD 70. It is recognized that one might argue the fact that since the three Synoptic Gospels record Jesus' prophecy between 27 and 30 AD - that the temple would be destroyed and assuming that these Gospels were written after AD 70, it would therefore be unnecessary to record the fact of the AD 7 destruction event. However, the reasonable response is that it would be even more compelling to reflect the fulfillment of Jesus' prophecy.

150	A book containing all of Paul's letters, except Titus and Timothy, is in circulation
150	Justin Martyr
156	Polycarp (7 -156) killed for failure to recant his belief in Christ.[10]
160	Irenaeus of Lyon (studied under Polycarp) canonizes the four Gospels
200	Earliest known compilation of all four Gospels published
221	Julius Africanus' History, referencing Thallus Codex Vaticanus and Codex Sinaiticus Bibles in existence
325	Council of Nicea under Constantine canonizes the entire New Testament
327	King Constantine, on visit to Jerusalem, seeks to have the Church of the Holy Sepulchre built near Golgotha, then located outside the city wall, and on top and around the tomb of Jesus
380	Roman Emperor Theodosius issues the edict of Thessalonica, which establishes Christianity as the official state religion. Even earlier, Christianity was made the official religion by Armenia and Ethiopia
390	Jerome's Vulgate Bible
401	Augustine's Confessions, Patricus taken into slavery, Germanic invasion of Roman Empire
432	Bishop Patrick arrives in Ireland
525	Dionysius: AD calendar
570	Mohammed born
632	Muhammed dies, Qur'an appears (alleged by Muhammad to have been largely dictated by the angel Gabriel)
691	Dome of the Rock constructed over site of Abraham/Isaac "sacrifice"
800's	AD calendar in general use
1291	Fall of Acre to Muslims
1384	Wycliffe's English Bible
1450	Guttenberg printing press (First book printed is the Bible.)
1516	Erasmus New Testament (Greek/Latin)
1517	Luther's "Ninety-five Theses," beginning of the Reformation
1522	Luther's NT (German)
1525	Tyndale's NT (English)
1539	English "Great Bible™ (Henry VIII)
1560	Geneva Bible (Colonial America's favorite)
1582	Gregorian calendar
1611	King James Bible (thanks to Tyndale who was burned at the stake in 1536)
1787	Ben Franklin prays for God's guidance at the Constitutional Convention
1948	After Jewish Diaspora commencing in 70 AD and enduring until 1948 when Israel was reestablished as a nation fulfilling Bible prophecy, and also prophecy that the Hebrew language would one day be re-established - a totally unprecedented event of language "resurrection!" ["For then I will return to the people a pure language that they may all call upon the name of the Lord to serve Him with one consent.' (Zeph. 3:9)] "You will know that I am the lord when I bring you back to the land of Israel, the land I had sworn to give to your fathers" [EZ 20:41, 36,28]
1961	A large stone was found in Caesarea inscribed: "Pontius Pilate, Prefect of Judea"

10. "Eighty- and six-years years I have served Him, and He hath done me no wrong. How can I speak evil of my King who saved me?"

Key Observed, Reported, and Recorded Facts and Events Surrounding Jesus's Crucifixion and Death

1. Relative to Jesus Christ's crucifixion, few people today question or even raise doubt as to whether Jesus Christ was in fact crucified. This includes the great majority of all scholars - believers and nonbelievers alike.

2. Relative to whether Jesus Christ in fact died on the cross, few people contend that Jesus did not die, and those who do offer no credible explanation of what happened to a severely wounded Jesus, what He must have looked like and how He survived if He did not die. The facts are clear that after was beaten severely over hours of time Jesus spent much of one day hanging suspended upon a cross with His arms outstretched and bones coming out of joint. The effect this has on the body's ability to breathe, particularly exhalation, after a very short time, is certain and devastating. Further, the reported and recorded observation of a Roman soldier piercing Jesus Christ's side and causing blood and water to gush out of Jesus's lungs is a telling detail that only God would record—not only for the detail but to demonstrate its scientific accuracy. Jesus's death was essentially the result of asphyxiation and hypovolemic shock. This caused His lungs to fill with fluid (pericardial and pleural effusion), which explains the gush of both water and blood from Jesus's side. Jesus's statement on the cross, "I am thirsty" is symptomatic of both hypovolemia and dehydration.[11]

   Note that the Roman soldiers broke the legs of many victims to expedite their deaths, but they did not need to do so for Jesus.

3. One of Jesus's seven phrases, spoken on behalf of his human side while He was on the cross, was "My God, my God why have you forsaken me?" (Matt. 27.46). If one were writing the story and seeking to falsely promote Jesus Christ as Lord and Savior, indeed as resurrected God, one would not likely choose to report a comment that would initially appear to many to be disingenuous, inconsistent, and even blasphemous—unless, of course, it was true and fully consistent with Jesus's being fully man and fully God.

---

11. See John 19:28 Also see chapter It in Lee Strobel's *The Case for Christ*, which sets forth the comments and opinions of Dr. Alex Metherell, a physician and engineer. I have known Dr. Metherell personally for a number of years, and his medical and scientific background, together with his long study of the Bible, qualifies him as an expert. His opinions eliminate all reasonable doubt as to the fact of Jesus's death on the cross. We must not fail to note the many incredible scientific truths that are contained in the Scriptures, two of which are captured here by the 'water gush' and "I am thirsty' facts. Both are thoroughly consistent with the symptoms of crucifixion.

   While there are many other scientific or medical examples, we note here two further examples. First, only in recent years has medical science discovered and confirmed that the human body's highest blood coagulability occurs on the eighth day of life. Is it any wonder that in the Old Testament God called for all Jewish boys to be circumcised on the eighth of life? (See Genesis 17:12.) Second, DNA was discovered only in recent years. DNA includes a precise and certain universal blueprint of man's genetic characteristics. It is a master blueprint that is so detailed, organized, systematic, and certain that it would be impossible to explain by evolutionary process. If one accepts the notion that DNA evolved, such willingness to place faith in a belief devoid of cognitive process is both whimsical and baseless.

4. Finally, the fact that Jesus was incarnated and came to earth primarily to serve as man's perfect sacrificial lamb and die for man's salvation is accepted by virtually all. One of the earliest phrases quoted and written (and tattooed!) after Jesus's death was "born to die".[12]

Old Testament Blood Sacrifice

From the earliest times in the Old Testament, God required bloodshed through the sacrifice of an animal offered to God as a substitutionary sacrifice for the redemption of human sins and atonement with God. "For the life of a creature is in the blood and I have given it to you to make atonement for yourselves ... it is the blood that makes atonement for one's life" (Lev. 17: n)

Why did God require this shedding of blood and substitution of life for life? Certainly, it was not because God had some strange or bizarre thirst for blood or death.

Rather, all of this was designed by God as a periodic reminder of people's sins and their need for redemption and atonement ("at-one-ment") with God. It was also meant to point ahead to the coming, ultimate, final sacrifice and shedding of blood that would take place with God's Son, Jesus. The shedding of Jesus's blood gave full and clear meaning to sacrificial death and the shedding of blood for one and all, once for all time.

Take note that God meant for this ultimate sacrifice and shedding of blood to be the last and final shedding of blood that would be necessary as a substitutionary sacrifice for all, regardless of race or nation. Each of us who personally accepts this sacrifice of Jesus's life as substitutionary on our behalf and in our place is thereby provided personal forgiveness of sin, justification, and atonement with God.

Then God went two steps further and *resurrected* Jesus, thereby providing the first resurrection. God promises a second resurrection: eternal life to all who accept Jesus's life sacrifice as substitution for their own lives. (See Genesis 4, 22.)

Cain and Abel

One other key point to note about this substitutionary blood sacrifice in the Old Testament is the fact that not just any sacrifice would suffice. Rather, the sacrificial animal, typically a lamb, had to be spotless and without blemish or defect, as perfect as possible. Why was this necessary?

Again, this was a forerunner to and a foretelling of the coming of Jesus Christ, the most wholly (and holy) perfect sacrifice possible. The fact that the final sacrifice and shedding of blood for all of mankind had to be through the most true and perfect sacrifice possible meant that it could only come through God's sacrifice of Himself through His Son, Jesus, as one person of the triune God. Thus, Jesus, being God incarnated as man, had to come to earth-first to teach and model the Christian life, and then to be our perfect sacrifice and die for us!

---

12. First, think of a time in your life when you were in pain, hurt, offended, upset, or unfairly or unjustly treated. Most often this was a consequence of your own action or conduct. Now visualize and meditate for a single minute of Jesus's experience in hanging on the cross in excruciating pain- pain totally undeserved-having never sinned or done anything wrong. He hung there, not because of his own conduct but for the misconduct and failures of all others, including you and me. After a moment or two of considering this, is it not true that your own pain, if not gone, has at least become bearable?

Cain's offer of a sacrifice to God consisted of farm produce and lacked the shedding of blood. Unlike Abel's sacrifice of an animal, Cain's offering was unacceptable to God. Cain went on to kill his brother Abel, and he was condemned to permanent death and separation from God.[13]

Abraham and Isaac

> *"Take your son - your only son, Isaac, whom you love, and go to Moriah.*
> *Sacrifice him there as a burnt offering on one of the*
> *mountains I will tell you about."*

The journey from Beersheba by Abraham and his son Isaac required three days. On the way Isaac asked Abraham,

> *"Where is the lamb for the burnt offering?"*
> *Abraham answered: "God Himself will provide the lamb!"*

Once Isaac was bound and laid on the altar on top of the wood, Abraham took his knife and raised it to slay his son. At that moment an angel called out to Abraham:

> *"Do not lay a hand upon the boy!"*

Abraham then saw a ram caught in the thicket, which Abraham and Isaac then sacrificed as a burnt offering to God.

Abraham called this place "The Lord Will Provide" - thereafter known as the "Mountain of the Lord," believed to be inside the Dome of the Rock on the Temple Mount.

God then, swearing by Himself, said:

> *"I will surely Bless you, and make your descendants as numerous as the stars in the sky."*

(See Gen. 22)

The most clear and dramatic precursor of the coming of Jesus Christ being a sacrifice for us is the incredible story of Abraham and his intended shedding of blood and sacrifice of his only son Isaac, the son promised by God and whom he had waited for until he was nearly a hundred years old. In obedience to God's command, and test of Abraham 's faith and trust in God, Abraham was about to shed Isaac's blood when God stopped him. Miraculously, God provided for Abraham a ram suddenly caught in nearby bushes, thereby providing an animal blood sacrifice for Abraham. As a result, God provided to Abraham what God would later deny to Himself, namely the prevention of the death of God's only son, Isaac. God's testing of Abraham found him totally obedient and trusting toward God. How many of us would have been or be found so? Praise God for not requiring such a difficult test of us! (See Genesis 22.)

After reading these stories in the Old Testament-which occurred and were written some two thousand years before Jesus's crucifixion, shedding of blood, and death-it would be difficult to conclude that anyone other than Jesus Christ, the Messiah, could ever be the perfect sacrifice for the sins of us all. Further, God's blood covenant and promise of resurrection were extended to all who would claim this substitutionary sacrifice of Jesus Christ as their own.

---

13.   See Genesis 4.

With today's high emphasis on self-esteem, self-pride, self-justification, and tolerance of all conditions and lifestyles, it's not so difficult for people to believe in the fact of the transforming process of Jesus's substitutional sacrifice. Rather, the difficulty is for people today to believe that they have a need for it![14]

Key Details of Reported and Recorded Evidence, Events, and Facts Regarding Jesus Christ's Resurrection

Take note that the facts and events along with the specific details surrounding Christ's resurrection lend high credibility and believability to the account. Consider the following eighteen examples.

1. Three outside environmental events, one of which is verified outside of Scripture, occurred as Jesus was dying on the cross.

   • A curtain, or veil, separated the innermost Holy Place from the rest of the temple in Jerusalem. The Holy Place was a sanctuary entered only by the chief priest on special occasions. It symbolized the "seat of God." While Jesus was on the cross, the veil was torn in two, down the center from top to bottom-the opposite direction in which such a curtain would be most likely to tear.

   • The ground shook, and many graves in the vicinity were suddenly opened, raising their contents from the dead.

   • The afternoon sun disappeared, and the skies were totally darkened for several hours throughout the Middle East and beyond.

Historian Julius Africanus (AD 221) referenced the works of historian Thalus (AD 52) in stating the following: "At the time of Jesus' crucifixion on the whole world there pressed a most fearful darkness; and the rocks were rent by an earthquake, and many places in Judea and other districts were thrown down...a darkness that appeared without reason. An eclipse of the sun takes place only when the moon comes under the sun; how then should an eclipse be supposed to happen when the moon is diametrically opposite the sun!" (See Africanus's and Thalus's report in _History of Eastern Mediterranean_ about an inexplicable darkening throughout the Middle East at the time of Jesus Christ's crucifixion.)

2. Jesus Christ made seven statements while on the cross

   • _"My God, my God, why have you forsaken me?"_ (Matt. 27:46).
   • _"Truly, I tell you, today you will be with me in Paradise"_ (Luke 23-41-43) (addressed to one of the two criminals being crucified beside him),[15]
   • _"Father, forgive them, for they do not know what they are doing"_ (Luke 23:34),
   • _"Dear Woman, here is your son; John, here is your mother"_ (John 19:26),
   • _"Father, into your hands I commit my spirit"_ (Luke 23:46),
   • _"I am thirsty"_ (John 19:28),
   • _"It is finished"_ (John 19:30),

---

14. "If we claim to be without sin, we deceive ourselves and the truth is not in us"(John I: 18). If we are not in Christ, "all our righteous acts are like filthy rags" (Isa. 64:6).

15. There is no punctuation in Hebrew. However, most Bible texts place a comma before "today" rather than after "today." Some could argue that the latter might be the correct placement. However, if in fact there is a separate "paradise" or holding place prior to heaven - and surely such a place is implied then the comma is correctly placed, and Jesus was saying that the crucified robber would be with Jesus in paradise "today" (Friday). The alternative is that Jesus was saying, "I tell you that you will be with me in paradise," i.e., eventually, when He returns for the rapture of the church and all others who are "asleep" in Christ, who will be resurrected first and will all then join Him in paradise - or heaven.

After reading the above seven statements of a man while suffering crucifixion on a cross con sider C.S. Lewis' comment that this could be no mere man - rather he had to be either a "lunatic," "liar," or "Lord".

Also take note of the Gospel's report of the statements made by two eyewitness observers while Jesus was on the Cross: the first being one of the two criminals hanging on crosses on either side of Jesus:

"Jesus, remember me when you come into your kingdom." (Luke 23:42);

The second, a Roman Centurion:

"Surely, he was the Son of God!" (Matt. 27:54)

3.   the body of Jesus Christ was placed in a tomb, not by any of his disciples or close friends, but rather by Joseph of Arimethea, a Sanhedrist who previously had been opposed to Jesus, and was reported a friend of Pilate. Jesus' enemies would thus have known well the location and could easily visit it.

4.   Jesus's body was wrapped in burial cloths along with one hundred pounds of spices, the weight of which alone could kill a person.

5.   A very large stone used to secure the entry to the tomb and the stone was sealed.

6.   Jewish leaders placed two guards at the tomb, fearing even the possibility that friends of Jesus Christ might steal the body.

7.   Matthew, at Mt. 28, reports that at dawn on the first day of the week Mary Magdalene and the other Mary went to the tomb and:

- "There was a violent earthquake"

- "An angel of the Lord came down from heaven, and going to the tomb, rolled back the stone, and sat on it"

- "The guards…became like dead men"

- "The angel said to the women…he (Jesus) is not here: he has risen, just as he said…" (also see Luke 24)

Thereafter, Jesus Christ first appeared to one woman, Mary Magdalene, and then two or three women, including Mary Magdalene, Mary, and/or Salome. They ran to tell Peter and John that the tomb was empty and that they had encountered a risen Jesus Christ.

In considering the above, recall that Old Testament Scripture always references the need for two or three witnesses to testify to any event or fact in any legal proceedings. Second, women were not regarded as credible witnesses, so these women were already disqualified as legal witnesses. If the apostles had been making up the resurrection story, there was no way they would have reported that women were the first witnesses to the resurrection, because no one would have been obligated to believe their account. Accordingly, the only reason to report that women were the first to come to the empty tomb is because it was true.

The Curse

8.   It was a curse to be hung on a tree. "If a man guilty of a capital offense is put to death and his body is hung on a tree, you must ... bury him that same day, because anyone who is hung on a tree is under God's curse" (Deut. 21:22-23).

It must already have been difficult for the writers of Scripture to record that woman were first to find Jesus's tomb empty and to be told by the angel that Jesus was risen. However, this difficulty pales in comparison to reporting that Israel's long-awaited Messiah-the one who was destined to conquer all of Israel's enemies (the Romans and others) and then assume David's throne-had (uh-oh) just been shamelessly hung on a tree(cross). Given this curse, Jesus's crucifixion would be the last thing any disciple would wish to report.

So why was Jesus's hanging on a tree not only reported but fully accepted by His disciples and others? It is simply because the impact of Jesus' crucifixion was totally transformed by the further fact - a fact even then widely accepted as true that on the third day, Jesus was resurrected, which meant that He was the true Messiah, the Christ![16]

The Folded Head Cloth

9.   Peter and John ran to the tomb and found the heavy stone rolled away. John in his eyewitness Gospel, and Luke in his expert report, both recount that upon entering the tomb, they found it empty and saw that Jesus' burial cloth for His head was neatly folded while the linen strips covering Jesus' body were undisturbed! Why would anyone include the detail of a neatly folded burial cloth, unless it was true? If someone had stolen Jesus' body, would they have neatly folded the cloth? Did any of the undisturbed linen strips become the Shroud of Turin?

Q: Why the detail of the "neatly folded" burial head cloth?

First, because it was a true and unusual detail observed by John. Second, because Jewish tradition was that if a diner's napkin was thrown down unfolded, the diner was finished; however, if the dinner napkin was neatly folded it signaled that the diner was not finished and would return - so too with the message intended by Jesus who promised to return. Third, if someone had taken or stolen Jesus' body – would they take the time to neatly fold the head cloth? Finally, as to the undisturbed strips of linen covering Jesus' body, one can wonder – if not conclude – whether one of these strips of linen contain the photo image imbedded onto the linen strip that Is the Shroud of Turin?

---

16.   While the church, for many reasons, has adopted Sunday as resurrection day, there can be no doubt that Jesus was in the tomb for three whole days and three whole nights, which was just as Jesus prophesied when He referenced the story of Jonah and the whale (Matt. 12:40). Many argue that a careful reading of the entirety of Scripture supports Jesus having been crucified and dying around 3 p.m. on Wednesday (the "Day of Preparation• before the annual Sabbath and then spending the three full nights of Wednesday, Thursday, and Friday and the three full days of Thursday (the high day Sabbath and the first day of the Feast of Unleavened Bread), Friday and Saturday in the tomb before rising at sunset on Saturday evening. Mark 16:19 states, "Now having risen, early the first day of the week He appeared first to Mary Magdalene." While the Greek has no punctuation, many interpreters have incorrectly placed a comma after "week" instead of "risen, which would tend to (incorrectly) support a Sunday morning resurrection. Therefore, when the women came to the tomb on Sunday morning, the guards were long gone, the stone had been rolled away, the tomb was empty, Jesus was not there (having risen at sunset on Saturday), and the angel(s) said, "Why do you look for the living among the dead? He is not here, he has risen." (Matt. 28).

The Two Guards and an Empty Tomb

10.   How does one explain the two guards falling asleep while guarding the tomb? Roman Guards were assigned to I of 4 watches - or only 6 hours. They typically remained standing or walking since falling asleep on duty meant punishment by death.

    It is most likely that neither - let alone both - of the guards fell asleep; rather it is most likely that both were "frozen" and made defenseless by the Lord during Jesus's resurrection. Scripture tells us that these guards "reported to the chief priests everything that had happened...and the Sanhedrin devised a plan; they gave the guards a large sum of money, telling them, "You are to say, His disciples came during the night and stole Him away... This is the story widely circulated among the Jews to this very day." (Matt 28: II -15)-And, indeed it is.

    What is clear is that Jesus's tomb was a tomb owned and provided by Joseph of Arimathea and that Jesus was buried by both Joseph and Nicodemus. The tomb was made secure by putting a seal around the large stone placed at its entrance, and the posting of guards. This tomb was found with the stone rolled away, and the tomb was empty! (Matthew 27:66). This fact remains undisputed, even by Jesus's enemies, both at the time, and still today.

    Know also that Jesus did not need to have the stone rolled away in order to escape the Tomb; thus, the stone being found rolled away was for the guards and us.

One can imagine the intense search effort that was conducted in an attempt to find the body of Jesus Christ. The search effort soon ended when no body was found, and there were many reports throughout the region of Jesus's resurrection and His appearances to many people over a period of some forty days. Indeed, it was clearly accepted by many, if not most, of the people at that time that Jesus Christ had in fact resurrected. Keep in mind that at that time-outside of the Jewish Pharisees or Saducees-many had no concept of resurrection, a resurrected body, or what it all meant. Perhaps this is true for many people today.

It is interesting to consider how the gospel writers might have learned that the guards had been bribed. Perhaps at least one of the guards was converted to "the Way," or Christianity.

One Bible critic who writes behind a pseudonym states he does not believe in Jesus' resurrection because "no one actually saw him rise", and that Jesus's "means of escape is a mystery". Since only Jesus was in the tomb, sealed and with a large stone, there may have been no witness to the actual resurrection itself, beyond the three witnesses of the Trinity, but I'm guessing that at least one of the two tomb guards will one day add interesting detail to the Gospel message!

As to Jesus's "means of escape" the critic chooses to simply ignore all of the vast and otherwise inexplicable evidence of Jesus's post-resurrection appearances, together with Jesus' Ascension which he notes is "not referenced by Matthew or John."

More Appearances

11.   The New Testament gospels and letters record that Jesus Christ, in addition to appearing to two or three women and the two men on the road to Emmaus, appeared in the upper room, first to ten apostles (Judas having killed himself) and then to the eleven, with doubt ing Thomas now present. Thomas, not unlike many of us today, would not believe until he had placed his fingers in the hole in Jesus Christ's side or in the nail holes of His hands and feet. In all, some eleven appearances are recorded in Scripture, and some are referenced in other historical reports. In truth, there were likely many more, given the forty days that Jesus remained on earth before His ascension.

- <u>Archeological Inscription Regarding Pilate:</u> An Italian archeologist, Antonio Frova, discovered in 1961 a Latin inscription at Caesarea on a stone which was being used as a part of the steps leading into the theater, reading in part:
  Tiberium - Pontius Pilate - Prefect of Judea. Historians Tacitus and Josephus referred to Pilate as "procurator," while the New Testament names him as "governor" (Matt. 27:2). It should be noted that this inscription is the only archaeological evidence discovered to date referencing both Pilate's name and title.

- <u>Archeological Inscription Regarding The Nazareth Decree:</u> In 1878 in Nazareth a stone was found inscribed with a decree from the Emperor Claudius (AD 41-54), likely issued following the riots of 49AD, prohibiting graves from being opened or moved, and mandating death for the offender. Emperor Claudius ' action was apparently in reaction to the reports regarding Jesus' tomb, keeping mind that the Sanhedrin explanation was that Jesus' body had been stolen by His friends.

A Small Miracle

12.   Jesus appeared to some of the apostles, who still not believing that Jesus was Messiah, had returned to their fishing occupation by the Sea of Galilee but were catching no fish. Jesus Christ told them to cast their nets on the other side of their boat, and upon doing so, they promptly caught fish. Once ashore, they counted 153 fish. None had been lost, for their net did not break (John 21:11). Why does this account include such detail, and why were there 153 fish?

The poet Oppian later reported in his "Catalogue of the Fishes," published in Halieutica, that at that time, there were known to be 153 varieties of fish in the world. John's gospel record of this fish-catching event was written between AD 85 and 90, and Oppian did not write his "Catalogue of the Fishes" until AD 190 during the reign of either Commodus or Severus. This is a small but dramatic miracle of Scripture that underlines the fact that all Scripture is inspired by God. Only God could have known in AD 85-90 what number of fish categories Oppian who was not yet born-would report more than a hundred years later in AD 190!

Why would a catch of 153 fish be otherwise significant? Because it illustrates that Jesus reaches out to *all-all* kinds, all varieties, all nationalities of people-with His message of salvation.

Once they are caught in the net of Jesus Christ, that net will not break. None of His sheep will be lost.[17]

Now, contrast this story in John with a similar story in Luke 5:6. This was a time when Jesus had not yet died and resurrected. He was about to select his apostles to be "fishers of men." Jesus instructed Simon and the other fisherman and apostles to cast their nets into the deep. This time, "such a large number of fish were caught that the nets began to break." (Do not be a fish who is initially attracted or entangled but then escapes Jesus 's net!)

13. We must not fail to see that Jesus Christ also chose this post-resurrection appearance at the Sea of Galilee to restore and redeem Peter by asking him three times, "Do you love me?" Jesus asked once for each of the three times people had asked Peter if he knew Jesus. While Peter had sat in the courtyard of chief priest Ananias where Jesus was being interrogated on the night before His crucifixion, three people had asked him, "Don't you know this man Jesus?" And each time, Peter had denied knowing Jesus-the very one to whom he had previously said, "You are the Christ" in response to Jesus's question: "Who do you say that I am?" (Mark 8:29; Luke 9:20).

---

17.   Jesus said, "I give them eternal life, and they shall never perish; no one will snatch them out of my hand (John10:28).

This is a story of understandable human weakness and cowardice. It is also a story of God's amazing grace, mercy, and power to regenerate, recreate, and forgive us when we fail-if we repent and turn to Him. (See also Luke 12:9.)

Note that Peter, in order to save himself, was quick to lie and deny Jesus _before_ Jesus had been crucified and resurrected. However, when Jesus's resurrection was personally confirmed to Peter, Peter did a complete turnabout. He preached to all about Jesus Christ "and him crucified and resurrected."

Further, when it came time for Nero and the Romans to kill Peter for his faith, Peter not only submitted himself to death, but he refused to be hung in the same fashion as Jesus Christ. Rather, he insisted that he be hung on the cross upside down. Imagine a person doing such a thing for something or someone if he had not witnessed or known the true, resurrected Christ! [18]

14. Many people saw Jesus Christ. They heard him, touched him, and saw him eat. Paul pointed out in 1 Corinthians 15:8, "Jesus Christ appeared to more than five hundred persons at one time-most of whom are still living." (And if they were still living at that time, they could have, and would have, spoken to many others, being thoroughly interrogated by the curious and the skeptic!)

As unique as such a resurrection was, Jesus's resurrection became well-known and accepted by many within this small community at that time. It is important to note that during this time, no one was known to have reported or recorded any falsity or doubt of the facts. It had been observed, reported, and known by many that (1) the tomb was empty and (2) Jesus had resurrected. His post-resurrection appearances were observed by so many that the resurrection was commonly accepted as true.

Finally, in this connection, note the following obvious, but often over-looked facts lending even greater credibility to the truth of Jesus crucifixion, death, resurrection, and multiple post-resurrection appearances:

- all of these events occurred within a very small, and the same geographical area in and very close to Jerusalem;
- all among the same knowledgeable people;
- additionally, most of these events occurred within a compact period of four to seven days, and all within forty days while Jesus remained on earth before ascending; and
- after His ascension there were no further reported, nor argued "illusions" or hallucinations," until Jesus' appearance to Saul some 3years or so later.

Convert the Enemy/Saul Becomes Paul

15. Jesus Christ appeared to Saul, an enemy of Jesus - next to Satan perhaps His chief enemy on the road to Damascus (Acts 9). Perhaps this was the single most impressive post resurrection appearance of Jesus Christ. Why did Christ appear to Saul? My military training and West Point experience help me to more fully appreciate the brilliance of Jesus as a strategist and tactician in choosing to appear to Saul. Saul was the foremost enemy of Jesus Christ. Articulate and highly intelligent, Saul was a strong leader and teacher of Pharisee¬ Judaism, and he was a principal persecutor of early followers of Jesus Christ.

---

18. One unidentified writer suggests that Peter was on his way out of Rome when he was suddenly confronted by Jesus Christ on the road. When Peter asked, "Lord, where are you going?" the Lord replied, "To Rome to be crucified." The astonished and embarrassed Peter immediately turned around, returned to Rome, and was arrested. It was then that he insisted on being crucified upside down (attributed to "The Acts of Peter. a very early but non-canonical book, "Who's Who in the Bible", by Readers Digest Assn. Inc., 1994. All of the apostles and close disciples, including Paul and excepting only John, gave their lives for a Jesus they had now seen and/or knew to be resurrected. See Chapter 2, FN.[4]

Acts 8:1 reports that Saul was present at - and was perhaps even the instigator of - the stoning death of Stephen, Jesus' first martyr. (Stephen was yet one more follower who professed Christ after Jesus' resurrection and then the first to give his life for his belief in 32 AD.) By converting Saul (renamed Paul), Jesus Christ eliminated the chief and most articulate opponent of the Christian faith, making Paul His chief witness.

The Thorn

One important postscript regarding God's frequent use of the "thorn in the flesh." Paul was indeed possessed of great personal talent, perhaps even charismatic. Add to that the special attention paid to Paul by Jesus himself and one can sense that human pride being chief among the deadly sins could have over-taken Paul, detracting from the Gospel message, away from Jesus and Him crucified. The answer for God- as is so often the case-was a dose of reality, humility and perspective- in this case an unidentified thorn in the flesh of Paul. Not only in allowing the thorn, but in refusing to grant Paul's three requests to remove it by saying: "My grace is sufficient for you, for my power is made perfect in weakness" (2 Cor.12:9). I submit that Paul's thorn is unidentified in scripture, so that greater and broader application can be made to the numerous pains we humans have-or as my mother would say- "the crosses we must often bear in our lives."

As we know, Paul would go on to write the first New Testament letters (to the Corinthians and Thessalonians). In total, he wrote thirteen of the twenty New Testament letters. During that time, he was persecuted and imprisoned on numerous occasions, yet he remained steadfast through out and "finished the race." Ultimately, he was beheaded under Nero for his faith.

The single fact that Paul-a highly educated, dedicated Jewish Rabbi, committed enemy of Jesus, and the poster child for strong will- could be turned 180 degrees by Jesus Christ's appearance is itself a compelling fact that has been responsible for converting more people, other than Jesus Himself. It is my opinion that it was because of Paul's strong will that Jesus blinded him for three days, during which time he fasted (Acts 9:9) After three days, Jesus told Ananias to "lift the scales" from Paul's eyes. This experience, followed by Jesus serving Himself as Paul's instructor for many days, and the additional days thereafter spent with the disciples, provided an intense time for impression, repentance, refocus, and the working of the Holy Spirit effectuating toward Paul's total reeducation and reorientation.

This event must persuade anyone with an open mind and even minimal experience with human nature of (1) the miraculous power of Jesus Christ and (2) the absolute fact of Jesus's resurrection, which was so clearly, directly, permanently, and indelibly witnessed by Paul, motivating Paul's subsequent life of sacrificial dedication and service despite much suffering.

16.   Let's look at two illustrations involving skeptics and committed evil doers.

The Skeptic and Changed Lives

If Paul was the poster child for having strong free will and being an enemy of Jesus, James, the brother of Jesus, was the poster child for skeptics. Not unlike Joseph 's jealous brothers, who tried to kill Joseph, James thought Jesus was his deluded older brother who talked strangely. James did not believe anything Jesus was saying. (One is never accepted as a prophet in his own hometown-or family.) However, following Jesus's resurrection, James instantly became a believer, assumed leadership of the Christian Church in Jerusalem, and was and was -- thrown down from the pinnacle of the Temple in Jerusalem and beaten to death with a fuller's club when he refused to deny Jesus. Also, perhaps not just James but also another brother of Jesus - made a 180 degree turn in support of Jesus' deity, post resurrection. (See l Cor9:5)

Also note that James told us in his New Testament letter, "What good is it, my brothers, if a man claims to have faith, but has no deeds?...Faith by itself, if it is not accompanied by action, is dead" (James 2:14- 17).

Among the many more recent and notable skeptics who were converted after investigation and study-skeptics who initially sought to disprove Jesus as the Christ-are Harvard Law School Professor of Evidence Simon Greenleaf, journalist and author Lee Strobel,[19] and attorney Chuck Colson, one of President Nixon's close advisors.

Study - Not Blind Faith

While the God-created conscience within each of us has certainly played a significant role in leading our hearts to be opened to the Holy Spirit and the way of Christ, I would submit that the human intellect once subordinated to God's wisdom and our God given free will-to be examined further later- plays the leading role by far.

The fact of the resurrection is not a feeling, emotional response nor blind faith; it is a conclusion based on search and study, utilizing our God-given intellect, reason, and our cognitive processes to seek God's wisdom in our assessment of all of the events, people and products of history together with the world around us.[20]

As such the following two observations are compelling

First, those who have decided not to believe or make a decision relative to Jesus Christ have rarely done so after thorough study and research of all of the material events, people, and products of history and the world around them, usually for one of the following reasons:

- refusal to engage in any study due to bias, prejudice, lack of diligence,[21] or a fear of the limiting effect it might have on their present life-style;

- electing to study only a selected portion of all the available information and data thereby being side-tracked to some belief, faith, cult, or practice other than Christianity; or

- failing to seek God's wisdom in their study.

---

19. See Simon Greenleaf's *The Testimony of the Evangelists. See Lee Strobel's The Case for Christ, The Case for Faith,* and other works.

   Of course, the single greatest product of history is the Bible (Basic Instruction Before Leaving Earth!). Note *Lincoln's* comment:

20. "I believe the Bible is the best gift God has ever given to man. All the good of the Savior of the World is communicated to us through the Book, but for it we could not know right from wrong."

   And *Immanuel Kant's*

   "The existence of the Bible, as a book for the people, is the greatest benefit which the h1:1man race has ever experienced."

21. Even Ben Franklin while believing in God, admitted in a letter written to Ezra Stiles in 1790 to not having taken the time to study whether Jesus' divinity was true or not.

Second, even more persuasive than the above is the fact that almost everyone who has thoroughly examined all of the material events, peoples and products of history along with the world around them, have concluded that Jesus lived, was crucified, was resurrected, is the Christ, and our living God, Creator, and Savior. Even more remarkable is that most of those who engage in this study start out as skeptics, agnostics, or even atheists!

Well-Known World Figures' Comments or References about God and/or Jesus after Study

Pilate's Wife to Pilate

"Don't have anything to do with that innocent man, for I have suffered a great deal today in a dream because of Him." Matt 27:19

Pontius Pilate

"I find no basis for a charge against this man." Luke 23:4
"I am innocent of this man's blood, it's your responsibility." Matt 27:24

One of the Two Criminals Hanging on Crosses on Either Side of Jesus

"Jesus, remember me when you come into your Kingdom." Luke 23:42

One of the Roman Centurion Guards at the Cross after Jesus Had Just Breathed His Last, and Suddenly the Skies Darkened, an Earthquake Occurred and Graves Opened:

"Surely, this man was the Son of God." Matt.27:54, Mark 15:39

Angel at the Tomb to the Women on Sunday Morning (following Friday's Crucifixion):

"You are looking for Jesus, the Nazarene, who was crucified... He has risen." Mark 16:6

The Sanhedrin Guards Outside the Tomb

The Guards reported to the Chief Priests "everything that had happened" at the tomb. (The guards were paid to officially report that his disciples came during the night and stole him away while we were asleep." (Matt 28:II-13)Talk about the original and only eyewitnesses to the very act of resurrection itself - it is these guards! Just imagine, hearing their witness once we get to Heaven!!

St. Thomas Aquinas 1225-1274

"There must be either a self-existent creator - or a self-existent universe, and the universe is not behaving as such."

Sir William Shakespeare (1564-1616)

"I believe, through the merits of Jesus Christ, my savior, to be made a partaker of Life Everlasting."

John Locke (1632-1704)

"There are some particulars in the history of our Savior...the principal of these is His Resurrection from the dead, which being the great and demonstrative proof of His being the Messiah...since the declaring His Resurrection was declaring Him to be the Messiah."

Sir Isaac Newton 1643-1727

"Gravity explains the motions of the planets, but it cannot explain who set the planets in motion. God governs all things and knows all that is or can be done."

Johann Wolfgang von Goethe (1749-1832)

"I look upon all four Gospels as thoroughly genuine."

Napoleon Bonaparte (1769-1821)

"I know men, and I tell you that Jesus Christ is not a man."

Lord Byron (1788-1824)

"If ever man was God, or God man - Jesus Christ was both."

Simon Greenleaf (1783-1853)

As Dane Professor of Law at Harvard University, Simon Greenleaf produced "the greatest single treatise on the law of evidence, "A Treatise on the Law of Evidence." Applying the same rules of evidence as administered in courts of justice, Greenleaf demonstrates the validity of the Gospels as trustworthy and authoritative historical accounts, stating:

"Let (the Gospel's) testimony be sifted, as it were given in a court of justice on the side of the adverse party, the witnesses being subjected to rigorous cross-examination. The result, it is confidently believed, will be an undoubting conviction of their integrity, ability, and truth."

Charles Dickens (1812-1870)

"I commit my soul to the mercy of God, through my Lord and Savior, Jesus Christ."

Leo Tolstoy (1828-1910)

"For thirty-five years I believe in nothing. Five years ago, my faith came to me. I believed in the doctrine of Jesus and my life underwent a sudden transformation. Instead of despair I tasted joy and Happiness that death could not take away."

Abraham Lincoln (1809-1865)

"I am profitably engaged in reading the Bible. Take all of the Book upon reason - and balance upon Faith; you will live and die a better man."

Lord Charles John Darling (1849-1936)

Lord Chief Justice of England: "There exists such overwhelming evidence - positive and negative, factual and circumstantial - that no intelligent Jury in the world could fail to bring in the verdict that the Resurrection story is true."

"Jesus: The Verdict," John Young

Albert Einstein (1879-1955)

"Certain it is that a ...rationality and intelligibility of the world lies behind all scientific work of a higher order...this firm belief...of a superior mind that reveals itself in the world of experience, represents my conception of God."

C.S. Lewis (1898-1963

Brilliant Oxford professor and author of "Mere Christianity," who after years of agnosticism, debate and study, wrote as follows:

"I am trying to prevent anyone's saying the really foolish thing...about (Christ):

'I'm ready to accept Jesus as a great moral teacher, but I don't accept His claim to be God.'

"A man who was merely man and said the sort of things Jesus said would not (merely) be a great moral teacher. He would be ...a Lunatic...the Devil (Liar)... or Lord and God."

Wernher von Braun (1912-1977)

The German Rocket Scientist, wrote:

"The vast mysteries of the universe should only confirm our belief in the certainty of the Creator."

"One cannot be exposed to the law and order of the universe without concluding that there must be design and purpose behind it all.'

Lee Strobel (1952-)

Lawyer and Investigative Reporter, and an atheist who, in his seeking to disprove God, was converted to Christianity, authored many books, including "Case for Christ," "Case for Faith," etc.

Committed Doers of Evil

Now, let's consider some notorious evildoers. The imprisoned Boston Strangler, Albert DeSalvo, was evil personified. Like thousands of others, his heart was regenerated when he became a believer as a result of the Great Commission. That is, he heard the Word and the gospel message, opened his heart to Jesus and was given a "heart transplant"-a regenerated heart-through the leading of the Holy Spirit.

Indeed, transformed lives are perhaps the best evidence-and perhaps the most convincing that most of us experience or see firsthand in our own lives: namely, the ongoing power of the resurrected and living Jesus Christ. This power of heart regeneration is something that only the Word and the power of Jesus and the Holy Spirit can offer. This power is available to all and has proven itself in the hundreds of thousands throughout human history who have opened their hearts to Jesus. As a result, they present themselves as living exemplars in the form of changed lives, redirected wills, and models of the love and peace of Jesus Christ. These changed lives can only be explained by newly regenerated hearts.

Most of us fall into this category of evildoers. Perhaps we are not so evil as King Herod, the Boston Strangler, or Adolf Hitler, but we are evil, nonetheless. If real and meaningful change is to occur, we need the power and ability of the Holy Spirit to secure for us hope, redemption (as was offered to Peter), renewal, and a new heart.

Miracles of Jesus

17.   Jesus performed a multitude of miracles, and the Gospels and other New Testament books record many of them. He multiplied the bread and fish to feed five thousand, an occurrence that involved so many people and was so broadly reported that it could not have been denied. He (temporarily} resuscitated people who had died, including Lazarus. Let us not do as Thomas Jefferson did and create our own version of the New Testament by eliminat ing all of Jesus's many miracles. We need only carefully observe the world around us and our experiences in life to recognize that miracles are real. The fact of Jesus's miracles is thoroughly consistent with His virgin birth and his having resurrected.

Shroud of Turin

18.   Is the Shroud of Turin one of the actual linen strips of cloth that covered the entire Crucified body of Jesus in the tomb.

> "*So, Joseph* (of Arimathca who provided Jesus' tomb) *bought some linen cloth, took down the body, wrapped it in the linen and placed it in a tomb*" (Mark 15:46),

> "*The other disciple (John} outran Peter and reached the tomb first. He bent over and looked in at the strips of linen. Then Simon Peter...saw the strips of linen lying there, as well as the burial cloth... folded up by itself, separate from the linen*" (John 20:4-7).

Today, the Shroud of Turin is in the Turin Cathedral in Turin, Italy, where it has resided for over four hundred years after previous residences in Jerusalem, Turkey, Constantinople, and France, and previously referred to as the "Image of Edessa." Many including the Catholic church believe it is the very linen cloth that covered Jesus ' body, and over his head (beneath the head cloth that would have been wrapped separately around his head) and then under his entire back and lying beneath his body.

What appears "unbelievable" is that this cloth has imbedded within or onto its fibers the photographic image of a nude male body, including showing injuries to the hands, feet, and side. It also has a face that bears strong resemblance to several famous early art images of Jesus. Most importantly, both the front and back images are "photographic negatives" - despite photography not yet having been invented! There is also evidence of blood residue (A-B) in various portions of the cloth, consistent with the precise wounds suffered by Jesus Christ's crucified body. Such a negative image could not have been painted onto or into the cloth by any known means...

In 1988 car bon -14 testing was performed, concluding that the age of the cloth was most likely somewhere in the period between AD 1000 and1500, contrary to other examinations that have concluded that the cloth is much older. Carbon-14 dating methodology is highly controversial and certainly imperfect. More recent, and very thorough carbon 14 studies have revealed that the 1988 tests had used a portion of the cloth that had been repaired in part and otherwise contaminated. Using other original portions revealed that the cloth was likely much older, and per haps even first century. (See *The Shroud of Turin and theC-14 Dating Fiasco* by Thomas W. Case, 1997.)

Reference is also made to a book entitled *Turin Shroud* by Picknett and Prince which suggests that the Shroud of Turin might have been a hoax created by Leonardo Da Vinci (1452-1519,) a highly talented but controversial character. However, until the eighteenth century when the shroud was sealed and placed under glass, the shroud was never displayed always having been kept care fully secured in its various locations. Investigation reveals no record of Leonardo's ever having seen the shroud let alone his ability to have the Shroud in his possession long before Leonardo was even born. Of course, if the shroud is a clever hoax by Leonardo, it would represent yet one more warning against placing one's faith in anyone or anything other than the revealed Word of God in Scripture. If the shroud is real, which seems highly probable, the unexplained photographic-flash "negative" effect - an effect that would most likely occur at the very moment Jesus' body was resurrecting would offer strong (maybe even undeniable) "photographic" evidence of a resurrecting Jesus. In any event, the shroud potentially remains a distinct piece of "real" evidence to be weighed in support of a resurrected Christ.[22]

Why did Jesus-Son of God - and God-have to die?

First, I would submit because so many feel need to ask the question!

Second, to illustrate just how much sin hurts both sinner and victim, sometimes even taking life

Third, the hurt, death or debt must be adequately punished - and death will be the only punishment to cover all sins for all mankind.

Fourth, punishment must be significant enough to be meaningful and effective, (ask any parent!)

Fifth, if I pay your debt, the larger your debt and the larger my payment, the more my love for you, and the greater your gratitude, relief and sense of forgiveness.

Sixth, Jesus/God did not kill another, He died Himself as God to show His incredible love for us, the seriousness of our sin, His willingness to pay a high price for our sin, and to focus our attention.

Seventh, to put real meaning into His forgiveness of us, and our forgiveness of others, forgiveness must be costly.

Eighth, to illustrate the majesty of not overcoming evil with evil, fear with fear, strength with strength, rather using humility and weakness, mercy, grace, and love to produce victory.

Ninth, to transform death into resurrection and life, and illustrating this with indelible impact.

Tenth, finally to quote John Stott: "when we sin, we substitute ourselves for God; when we are forgiven, God substitutes Himself for us"

Eleventh, being created in God's image we seek – in our inner spirit – genuine *love* and true *justice*.

Also, see FNs

This will be relatively free and is often very strong. Ever since the fall of man in the Garden of Eden, the heart is naturally human and is inclined to be oriented to self rather than God.

Love can often be less than true or genuine – sometimes masquerading as mutuality of respect or caring ["Let us not love with words or tongue but with actions and in truth" (I John 3:18). Genuine love can have no better definition than that provided by Jesus – "Greater love has no one than this, that he lay down His life for His friends." (Jo 15:13)] This is precisely what God and Jesus did this for each of us!

Justice: As a trial lawyer I can tell you that real and meaningful Justice in the world is often sought, but rarely achieved. You know this well in your own experience – be it an issue of large or small significance. Compare this with God's Justice that is pure, true, and complete, whether in small or large matters. This is the Justice we must seek for our sins against our Holy, Pure, Loving and Just God – who despite our sin and filth still seeks to save us to the extreme of giving His own life for us and in our place! Just, as Peter reacted when Jesus explained that He must wash the feet of Peter – Peter said – "Lord, wash not just my feet, but all of me" – so too we must say, " Lord, take all of me," seeing our own Death as not only Just, but a willing sacrifice we should want to offer to God, thereby substituting our sinful self for the Holy and Righteous Spirit and Cloak of Christ.

4

The Ascension of Jesus Christ, the Great Commission, Free Will, Freedom, and the Return of Jesus Christ

Why, after His resurrection and His appearances over a period of forty days, would Jesus Christ leave earth and ascend from the Mount of Olives to heaven?

First, though Jesus left earth, He left in His place the Holy Spirit and comforter, the third person of the Trinity. Jesus said this was "better," in that the Holy Spirit could be everywhere, with and within each and all of us, at one time-unlike Jesus, who was at one place or with one person at a time (John 14:16-17).

Second, Jesus left to "prepare a place" for all who eventually come to Him. He will return to gather them in rapture at a future time, a time that grows closer and closer. In the meantime, Jesus Christ leaves the Holy Spirit and people to utilize human will[1] to decide to "come to Him" by opening their heart's door, that decision itself being a gift of God. Once having done so, con verts are invited to join Jesus's church army as His soldiers and disciples to carry out His Great Commission.

Third, it would be easier for Jesus Christ to simply make puppets of each and all of us and "force" us to come to Him. As He did with Paul, Jesus could appear to each of us individually! Despite the impact, importance, and purpose of Paul's experience, for Jesus to force His will on us would be totally meaningless and of no value to us, God, or His purpose. Rather, God created within each human being an independent will. God seeks and desires that each of us-through the exercise of a will that is strongly inclined toward a "human nature" that is averse to God- to decide to open the door of our heart to Jesus.

God allows trials and tribulations into our lives so He can use them to awaken us and bring us to Him. As children disciplined by a loving Father, we should welcome life's painful trials.[2]

1.　This is relatively free and is often very strong. Ever since the fall of man in the Garden of Eden, the heart is naturally human and is inclined to be oriented to self rather than God.

2.　"And we know that in all things God works for the good of those who love Him, who have been called according to His purpose" (Rom. 8:28). "Consider it pure joy ... whenever you face trials of many kinds, because ... testing of your faith develops perseverance ... be mature" (James 1:2-4).

It is a fact that we often do not choose to open the door to our heart until we find a need to do so. That need is often produced through life's setbacks, failures, trials, pain, suffering, and other events and experiences that point us toward Him. Whether out of desperation, as a last resort, through prompting by the Holy Spirit, or by hearing the gospel at a time when our "soil" has been made fertile, our hearts can be opened, and God's purpose accomplished![3]

In fact, the heart is regenerated through the work of the Holy Spirit, and our new spirit "motor" fills us with a new desire-or even compulsion-to serve God. However, if our new heart acts like a motor, it is the mind that functions like a steering wheel. The mind must be refocused on, or transformed to, the things of God. The computer acronym GIGO means "garbage in, garbage out." So it is with our minds, which must feed on God's Word.[4]

Through circumstances, events, the work of the Spirit, and the exercise of our wills, our lives are changed. Through the "domino effect" of our Christ -inspired actions and deeds, human relationships and conditions in the world are changed. This is the result of our emulation of Jesus's character and the Holy Spirit's indwelling of us. Jesus taught His disciples- and us--to do these things:

- Have a grateful heart and a humble spirit.
- Sacrifice and give of our God-given talents, time, and treasure to others.
- Love God first, and then all others, more than self;
- Be peacemakers.
- Turn the other cheek; payback no wrong for wrong.
- Be servants and provide servant-leadership.
- Forgive others.
- Trust Him, not ourselves.
- Rid ourselves of self-pride and idol worship.
- Encourage one another and build each other up.
- Give thanks in all circumstances.
- Pray continuously.

---

3.   As a result of the fall of man, our hearts are slaves that have become bonded to sin. They are pre programmed toward our sinful, human nature and away from God. At the same time- but for a time only- Satan, the Prince of the Air, is being allowed by God to reign relatively freely in the world. Together with his demons (one third of the stars of heaven (angels) who fell out of the sky along with Satan), he encourages evil, self-pride, idol worship, and self-interest in the human heart. (See Revelation 12:4-9.)

The only way to reprogram our hearts is to regenerate or renew them (or "reboot" them, for the techies) by opening our hearts to Jesus and allowing the Holy Spirit to take control over our sinful nature. In doing so, we become bonded to God and are now slaves to Him. (I have often thought it interesting that "live" spelled backward is "evil." Perhaps it is a warning to all of us not to live backwards.)

4.   "Do not conform to the pattern of the world but be transformed by the renewing of your mind. Then you will be able to test and approve God's will" (Rom.12:2)

The Christian's faith is activated and actuated through selfless deeds and service to others. Critical institutions and all manner of charitable organizations and world outreach missions such as the Salvation Army, World Vision, the Red Cross, and so forth-have been established by Christians. The forerunners of most of today's large hospital systems were founded by Christian churches. All of these have had incredible impact in providing love and care for those in need of care in the world. None of this would have occurred if not for the discipling process of changed hearts and minds in the service of Christ and the fulfillment of His Great Commission.[1]

Add to this God's patience, love, and desire that "none should perish" but that all should come to Him, and you begin to understand-and be eternally grateful for-Jesus Christ's delay in His return and the day of judgment. This gives us and all of our loved ones more time to learn to love, to become fertile "soil," and to open our hearts to God's Word, thereby illustrating to the world the truth and the only way to salvation and peace.

Jesus's objective is to first receive each of us who turns away from evil and comes to Him as His child. Then He charges each of His disciples with the Great Commission: to spread the good news of peace, love, and salvation to others. Isn't this the most powerful, impactful, and meaningful way to spread the gospel? First, He creates as many disciples as possible. Then He energizes these many disciples to witness and spread the good news to others. There is nothing like "word of mouth" and firsthand witnessing of life's experiences to enhance credibility and believability. It is also yet another strong and effective "God strata gem" to overcome and conquer the Enemy "from within," which is, perhaps, particularly effective in this "wired" age.

Trusting in God

We cannot "have our cake and eat it too." Likewise, we cannot serve two masters. Thus, we can not love both Jesus Christ and the world. It is not enough to simply know with our minds or intellect that Jesus is in fact the Messiah/Christ, our Savior and Creator. We must also love and obey His Word, and He (not ourselves) must be the Lord and master of our lives. As children of God, we must live in the world, but we do so as citizens of heaven traveling through the world. As we travel, we are laying up eternal, not earthly, treasures (our souls, character, knowledge of God's Word, prayers, and all of our experiences reflecting God's Word and love to others) for our heavenly home.

While God's blessings-as with sunshine and rain- fall on all, it is critical to understand that only God's children-those who have accepted and serve Jesus as Lord-possess an array of gifts. Here are some of the gifts God gives His children:

- Forgiveness of sins
- Righteousness and justification
- Reconciliation and atonement with God
- Eternal salvation and freedom from death
- Protection from the coming great tribulation in the world
- Direct communication with God through prayer
- The armor of God and protection against the unseen, but very real, evil spiritual realm Inner peace and joy that "passeth all understanding"
- Protection of guardian angels

---

1.   "We are...created in Christ Jesus to do good works" (Eph. 2:10).

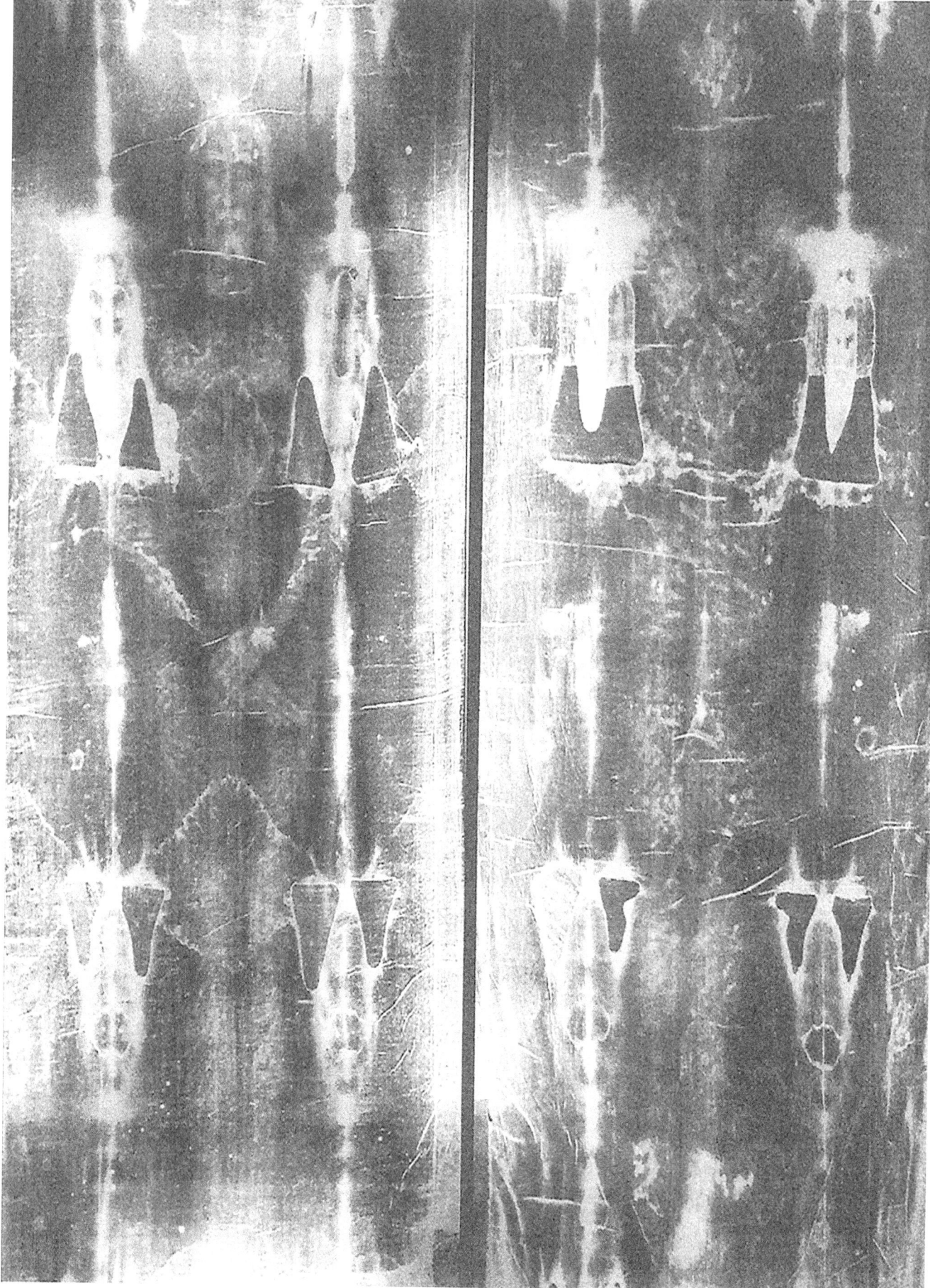

- The eternal presence of Jesus Christ and the power of the indwelling Holy Spirit and comforter in and through all of life's trials and tribulations
- The promise that "in all things God works for the good of those who love Him, who are called according to His purpose" (Rom. 8:28)
- Knowledge of true meaning and purpose of life

Meaning of Life

Who does not search for the true meaning of life? Here it is, right before our eyes and ears!

Jesus told us –

> *"I am the way, the truth and the life. No one comes to the Father except through me "(Jn 14 :6)*
> *"For God so loved the world that he gave his one and only Son, that whosoever believes in him shall not perish but have eternal life". (Jn 3:16)*
> *"I and the father are one." (Jn IO: 30)*

Who could possibly know and say such things-liar, lunatic, or our Lord?

Free Will and Freedom

We have noted that God created man with a will-a very strong will that enjoys relative freedom. Jesus taught us the true meaning of being free, and He did it, interestingly, at a time when slavery and many forms of servitude were commonplace. To be truly free, we must first be free from the bondage of sin. Jesus understood this, and He offers us the only means of ridding ourselves of our bondage to evil: by replacing it with bondage to what is good, through Him and the Holy Spirit who infuses our heart. As a result, we can only experience true freedom by first restraining our freedom to sin. Then, as we all learn through experience, true freedom can only work if we first acknowledge our obedience to, and our trust in, a loving and holy God.

Accordingly, no concept of freedom arose with Plato, Socrates, or Aristotle, who taught that the State is the highest authority and that the individual must first be subject and obedient to the State. Neither did any concept of freedom come from the Romans, who taught in a fashion similar to the philosophers.

Neither did freedom arise out of the French Revolution, an Orwellian movement leading only to tyranny. Nor did it originate in the AD 600s with Muhammad, whose Qur'an contains not a single reference to individual freedom or free will. Rather, it insists that all become followers or be subject to death.

Likewise, the idea of being free was not born in Great Britain, whose kings during the Middle Ages were the ultimate authority. All law, including the parliament, was subject to the king's edicts. God surely used this situation for good, as it caused the Puritans, Pilgrims, and others to leave Britain and travel to America in an attempt to gain religious freedom. This eventually resulted in the founding of a nation designed to be a new experiment. Men would be governed in what all hoped would be relative freedom, and at the least, they would have religious freedom.

However, neither did freedom originate in 1789 with America's founding nor in 1791 with the first amendment of the US Constitution, which set forth our individual freedoms-including religious freedom or even individual freedom which remains the subject of much controversy to this day.

Perhaps only now, in this postmodern age and latter stage of the "American experience," do we begin to understand that for all to enjoy true freedom in the sense intended by God, we must first limit our freedom by pledging ultimate obedience to a loving and holy God. The alternative is obedience to the rule of self, man, majority rule, or representative government- all made up of men. Do we need any more evidence that placing our trust and obedience in unloving and unholy hands will only limit our freedoms and create unfairness, ill treatment, prejudice, inequality, abuse, and all forms of evil, which only ultimate rule by a loving and holy God can eliminate?[2]

God's love for freedom and for His people to be free and live-in peace could not be better illustrated than by all of the amazing steps He took to free Israel from bondage in Egypt. As suggested elsewhere in this book, yet to be experienced in the coming years will be the extent to which God will go in His desire for Israel's protection and peace in the world of today.

The following Scriptures refer to the origination of the concept of freedom:

"In my anguish I cried to the Lord; he answered by setting me _free_" (Ps. II8:5, emphasis added).

"I will walk about in _freedom_, for I have sought out your precepts" (Ps. n9:45, emphasis added).

"The spirit of the Sovereign Lord is on me, because the Lord has anointed me to preach the good news to the poor...to _proclaim, freedom_ for the captives" (Isa. 61:1, emphasis added).

"Now the Lord is the Spirit, and where the Spirit of the Lord is, there is _freedom_" (2 Cor. 3:17, emphasis added).

"If you hold to my teaching ... then you will know the truth, and the truth will set you free" (John 8:31- 32, emphasis added).

"So, if the Son sets you _free_, you will be _free_ indeed" (John 8:36, emphasis added).

"It is for _freedom_ that Christ has set us free... [from] a yoke of slavery" (Gal. 5:1).

"The perfect law that gives _freedom_..." (James 1:25, emphasis added).

---

2.   Samuel, a prophet of God, told us in I Samuel 8 about the consequences that man will be subject to when he chooses to be ruled by men (or a king) rather than by God, and how man's rule can only result in greatly restricting the freedoms of all. Both the few and many will greatly limit and burden the freedoms of others. These lessons are more manifest today than ever before, both in America and the world at large.

Elimination of Prejudice and Inequality

Just as Jesus came to bring "sight to the blind", so too he came to blind all of us to prejudice and inequality based on race, nationality, gender or status.

Children of God and Sons of Christ are clothed with Christ. "There is neither Jew nor Greek, slave nor free, male nor female, for you are all one in Christ Jesus." [Gal. 3:28]. Children of God are incapable of prejudice or inequality; each and all are seen as one.

Jesus has also taught us to love one another, and in fact, "in humility consider [all] others better than yourselves." [Phil. 2:3]

Many in the world today have logically concluded that to practice prejudice and inequality is impractical, not political, or not conducive to their own well-being, and have therefore "willed" themselves to at least act in a fashion that is seen as without prejudice or inequality. While such conduct is a step in the right direction, it does not come from the heart, and it is not motivated by God's love.

Prejudice and inequality are but two more sins within the evil heart, and without heart regeneration and the Holy Spirit's guidance, the potential for prejudice and unequal treatment will always be present. Teaching and preaching helps but in themselves will never solve the problem or rid people of the sin of prejudice and inequality

Once again, the way to eliminate prejudice and inequality is clear, and perfect, and there is only one way. It is the way taught 1,985 years ago by a 33-year-old Jewish man when he said:

Christian Exclusivity?

Like many teens, I imagined myself to be totally incapable of prejudice, injustice, inequality, unfairness, etc., and I was impressed by those who charged Christianity as being "exclusive" and maybe a bit "snobbish" in taking the position that Jesus was the only way to the Father and eternal salvation. The argument proceeded to say, "it's unfair" and "what about other religions" and "what about those in the world who have never hear the gospel message" and so on[3]

After opening my heart to the Lord following the suicide death of my earthly Father and as a result of seeking God's wisdom[4]- not mine nor man's-I would offer the following responses to all of these exclusivity claims.

---

3.   Actually, the Gospel message is often seen, not heard!

4.   We can all have intelligence, but true wisdom comes only from God. "If any of you lacks wisdom, he should ask God who gives generously to all without finding fault, and it will be given to him" (James1:5)

   For the message of the cross is foolishness to those who are perishing, but to us who are being saved it is the power of God. For it is written...

   "I will destroy the wisdom of the wise, the intelligence of the intelligent I will frustrate" (1 Cor. 1:18,19).

   Accordingly, note that it is not our "worldly wisdom" that will lead us to the Christ, but God's wisdom and God's leading through the Holy spirit only-so that no one can boast, except in the Lord. (See I Cor. 1.)

   Accordingly, note that it is not our "worldly wisdom" that will lead us to the Christ, but God's wisdom and God's leading through the Holy spirit only-so that no one can boast, except in the Lord. (See I Cor. 1.)

1.   A true God must be both Loving and Holy and such a God would certainly choose to reveal himself to the world, doing so at a propitious time in world history.

> How better to meaningfully reveal oneself than to be incarnated, and living among the people for 33 years?[5]

> How better to prove one's Holiness than by a virgin birth, and dying for the sins of the world?

> How better to prove identity than by Resurrection after death, followed by Jesus's Ascension and the coming of the indwelling Holy Spirit?

A propitious time would not be at the beginning nor end of mankind, nor at any time when the events would be unknowable, ignored or lost.

Thus, the chosen time was roughly in the middle of mankind's history, in the geo graphical middle of the world and world civilization at the time, and a time of relative peace "Pax Romana" and means of travel over Roman built roads.

Did not all of the above incredible and special historical events occur? Are/Were they not each truly unique and from one source?

In addition to all of the above would not a Holy, Just and Loving God reveal Himself and His guidance to us through direct and express communications advising us how to live and act?

Thus-

- God's infallible "word" to us - the Bible:
- Basic Instruction Before Leaving Earth!
- <u>Prayer</u>: Direct line of communication between God and His Children;
- <u>Angels</u>: (remember the important unseen in God's creation) who carry communications and help to us from God; recall Gabriel's appearances to Mary, Joseph, et al;
- <u>Dreams</u>: Recall just a few of God's numerous occasions of communicating through dreams to or through: Joseph, Abraham, Jonah, Daniel, and on and on. [Of course, most dreams, like most TV channels are totally uninfluenced by God!

Finally, to those who object to a Holy and Just God [instead desiring only a God of "Love", ignoring how wicked man can choose to be] does not God trump all by His greatest act of love, i.e., by forgiving anyone for everything in sole return for our accepting the Son of God's death in our rightful place? As such we surely do have a "Loving All" God!

2.   If there is only *one true God*, it seems logical that there should be only one true *way* to God, and only as He determines.[6]

3.   There is and has been only one Son of God, the Christ, who was incarnated and came to earth to teach us and show us *the* way to the Father.

---

5.   Dream = Deity Reaching Earthlings About Mission
6.   Truth = The Reality Uncovered Through Him

4. The way is singular, _exclusive_ of no one-rather it is all inclusive, being open to all-to each and every one of us. It is totally fair, requires no unattainable requirement or circumstance, and is not based on any condition of birth, nationality, station of life, stature, economic status, or deeds, performed. In fact, children of God are totally blind to these things

5. _The way is not forced_ on us, and it is not based on unreasoned or irrational decision-making, blind faith, or emotions. Rather, it requires the exercise of our individual and free wills and requires application of our cognitive function to process, assess, and evaluate facts and events-and to be open to the leading of the Holy Spirit.

6. God tells us, "My ways are not your ways." Who are we-the creatures-to question the way(s) of the Creator? In fact, we must forget "our" ways!

7. Remember that Christianity is not just another "religion." It is a unique relationship with a singularly unique person, the only Son of the one and only God. By its very nature, this relationship must be unique and singular, but otherwise it is "all inclusive."

8. Finally, while our acceptance of the substitutionary life sacrifice of Jesus is the primary way for us to secure salvation and be assured that one has received salvation, take note that our loving God:

   • has also promised salvation for those who never heard the gospel message but who placed their faith in God under the Abrahamic covenant, and
   finally, has also promised to have "mercy upon whom I will have mercy and ... compassion on whom I will have compassion" (Ex. 33:19). Scripture references those who have come to know God through His created order, nature, con science, etc., in Romans I and 2.

Each spring brings renewal and new life. Seeds that were buried begin to rise and grow into new life. God surely intends this to be nature's sermon on resurrection, renewal, and regeneration. I have often thought that one of God's greatest double meanings is in the daily rising of the sun, which remind us that as the sun rises, so did His Son rise

Answering the Question of Christ's Resurrection

America's system of Justice is based on an adversarial approach, with each side of a case being represented by legal counsel opposing each other, with each side advocating its strong points and attacking the opponent's weaker points.

Note well that God has ordained a similar, adversarial system to exist in the world. While Jesus following His Ascension and until His return has taken on the role of Counsellor to plead the case of each of His follower-clients in the Court of Holy God in Heaven, Jesus has left us with the Holy Spirit to serve each of us as Counsel here in the World to advocate the case of Christ. Opposing counsel in the world's courtroom is, of course, Satan, whose primary tactic is to put forth all manner of lies - and only lies - in attacking the opposing case of Christ and His followers.

Each of the facts presented in this book are supported by one or more of the forms of evidence and methodology accepted in our courts of law, including:

• Ancient creeds or documents;
• Official records;
• Records maintained in ordinary course of business;
• Eyewitness testimony;
• Expert opinions;

- Statements or evidence based on dying declarations, present memory, past recollections recorded, exclamatory statements and *res gestae*; and
- "Real Evidence" (e.g. the "Shroud of Turin?")

We submit that any jury panel of twelve [originating from the 12 Apostles of Christ] open minded laymen considering all of the facts and evidence, including any and all contrary arguments, would conclude that Jesus was in fact resurrected. Further, we submit this conclusion would result whether the burden of proof was based on a mere preponderance of evidence, rea sonable probability, a clear and convincing standard or beyond any reasonable doubt as required for US criminal law cases.

Elsewhere in the book we have referenced several highly experienced lawyers, law professors and jurists who have considered this subject and all are in agreement with our conclusion.

Of course, each of us must study and answer for ourselves the question of whether Jesus was in fact resurrected and was the Messiah-Christ.

In doing so it should be noted that like with most events in history involving multiple humans there will be some variations in the details of reported observations. However, unlike most cases and controversies, virtually all of the relevant and material evidence that exists here reflects near total unity and consistency. Further it is virtually free of all bias[7] and is lacking in any significant or reasonable contradictions or alternative explanations.[8]

Whether considering all (or none) of the evidence, should one elect not to believe that Jesus was resurrected, note well and solemnly that such nonbelief does not, and obviously cannot change the *fact* as to whether Jesus was resurrected. Accordingly, in one's nonbelief, one acts at one's own peril with total inability to escape the all-encompassing and eternal consequences of such nonbelief.

Of course, if we conclude that the resurrection of Jesus is a fact, then we need to further under stand and accept the incredible consequences of Jesus Christ's resurrection - what it means to each of us and to our souls, both here in this present world - and for all of eternity.

- Jesus is alive today and forever.
- Jesus is the Messiah. He is Jesus the Christ.
- Jesus is the Son of God, and He is God-a triune God in three parts: God the Father, God the Son, and God the Holy Spirit.
- There is only one God, the triune God.
- Jesus Christ is the truth and the only way to the Father, to forgiveness of sin, to salva tion of the soul, to a resurrected body, and to life eternal.

---

7. Indeed, the only bias involved is a reverse bias and interest: namely despite the primary interest of each human is self-survival [i.e., saving one's own neck], but excepting only John, who was imprisoned on Patmos, all of Jesus' Apostles - including Paul - submitted to death rather than deny Christ's resurrection. Who would possibly do this for what they knew to be a lie, or a mere hope, presumption, or belief?

8. Some few, including Muhammed, argue that Jesus did not die. Some believe that He was later resuscitated. Alternatively, some may believe that Jesus died, was not resurrected, and did not appear in bodily form, arguing that all the "resurrection" witnesses were experiencing illusions or suffering from hallucinations. I say to them, show me credible evidence - or any credible evidence. Interestingly, the Qur'an suggests two possible explanations in lieu of acknowledging Jesus' death:(r) a substitution (perhaps Judas) in place of Jesus on the cross; or (2) some miraculous escape or rescue allowed Jesus by Allah - followed by Jesus' ascension while yet alive to heaven.

- Jesus is unique but not exclusive. He is open to all. He uses not force but rather facts, evidence, the working of the Holy Spirit, and the gift of faith to persuade our very strong and free wills to open our hearts to accepting Him.
- If and when we redirect our will and open our heart to accept Jesus, the Holy Spirit enters in, our human heart is "regenerated," and we become "reborn."[9]
- This heart regeneration can only occur through the indwelling Holy Spirit, which is a gift of God.[10]
- With rebirth, the Spirit within us creates and causes (it can do nothing else!) an over whelming love for Jesus; a compelling desire to know, obey, and serve Him; and a desire to model one's life after Him in both word and action, with the result that one's life can not help but bear fruit, like a branch in a grapevine bears grapes.[11]
- With rebirth, we become children of God where there is "neither Jew nor Greek... slave nor free... male nor female", where we consider others better than ourselves, and where practice of prejudice or inequality is not possible.
- In rebirth, each new disciple receives the Great Commission and helps effectuate God's kingdom and will here on earth. We recognize that we will fall well short of the perfection that can only be realized under God's reign when heaven finally arrives here on a new earth.
- Finally, if Jesus was resurrected, He was the first resurrection. You, your children, and your grandchildren-together with all others who are in Christ or are elected to come to Christ before life's end-will be part of the "second" resurrection. Accordingly, it is by this means, and this means only, that we, our children, and our grandchildren can be assured of receiving peace, freedom and equality, meaningful protection, permanent salvation, a resurrected (and perfect) body for all of eternity and being prepared and knowing our destiny!

The Mere Fact or Event of the Resurrection Itself

One final illustrative point using man's mere reason and logic, totally absent of and apart from all of the hard evidence and facts in support of resurrection as set forth in this book:

Pretend you are God (always dangerous, but just this once!) and as God - and "I am" - please assume the following facts:

- I am all Loving, but also Holy and Just;
- I have given to each of my creations - both angels and men - a free will - which I will not violate;
- As a result of Satan's free will, he chose to be his own God; mankind has followed, and all have sinned and were born in sin;

---

9.   See Nicodemus's meeting with and question to Jesus: "How can I possibly be born again?" (See John3 :1- 19.)

10. God is spirit and the source of all spirit. While the following is oversimplification for sure, metaphorically picture God's spirit as gasoline, the human heart as a gas tank inside the human body (car), and the human body as the car that requires spirit (gas) in order to run properly and permanently. In order to get this spirit (gas), the human(car) needs the long hose of the Holy Spirit to be inserted into the human heart (tank), thereby infusing the spirit (gas) into the heart (tank). Once infused with the spirit of God, the heart can be redirected toward God and His work.

11. Take caution: mere "acceptance" of Jesus with our lips is insufficient. As R. C. Sproul puts it so well: "We cannot confess what we don't first possess." We must avoid being the barren branch in the grapevine, which the great gardener will prune and is destine d for the fire!

- Being Holy and Just, sin must be punished, and the penalty of sin is death-no exceptions;
- I have created a Heaven where all righteous men can live for eternity- absent all death,
- sin and evil.
- Being a Loving and Merciful God - I desire none - no not one - to perish, and for all to inherit
- Eternal Life with me in Heaven, unless by the exercise of one's inviolable free will, one chooses to ignore or reject my desire and my plan for repentance, justification, salvation and eternity;
- For one to be justified, wholly innocent blood must be shed with suffering, and death must occur;
- As God I can accomplish each and all of these objectives by only one plan or means.

OK, now applying as only you or I can, not the mind of God, but our mind, the mind of man, what is the plan? Of course, no man could create or even imagine such a plan, only God! Further, it is/was only after the resurrection of Jesus, the Messiah-Christ, that we learned of God's plan.

Indeed, not one of the Apostles believed or understood the plan ahead of the Resurrection (remember they all ran and hid after Jesus' crucifixion!) despite the fact that Jesus had told them the plan several times:

- "the son of man will be flogged, crucified, and on the third day raised to life" (Mark 10:34; Matt. 20:19)
- "the son of man must be killed and on the third day raised to life." [(Mark 8:3); Matt.16:21]
- "the son of man - they will kill him and on the third day He will be raised to life." (Matt. 17:23)
- "destroy this temple and I will raise it again in three days." (Jn 2:19)

Further, most people even today, 2,000 years later, cannot (or choose not to) accept the plan!

In any event no man has ever imagined or forecast God's Plan; like most of God's marvelous creations and blessings, man is totally incapable of either conceiving or imagining such things. And, this is our point. Such a plan could only have been the plan of a Creator - a Holy, Just and Loving God - and a plan designed before even the outset of man's creation.

"I will give you a New Heart and put a New Spirit within you; I will remove from you your heart of stone and give you a heart of flesh – and I will put my Spirit and move you to follow my decrees and be careful to keep my laws" [EZ 36:26]

Accordingly, the very act and fact of such an incredible plan is in itself self-evident and self-proving of God, and ultimately the fact of the resurrection itself - all without resorting to any of the overwhelming facts and evidence presented in this book.

God's Plan

The existence of a Triune God, to include the Son of God being incarnated for 33years, born of a virgin, and being the Messiah-Christ.

God's Son, being both God and man was wholly sinless and a perfect sacrifice for the sins of man.

Allowing sinful man in the exercise his free-will see, experience and receive God's

incredible love for us, to repent, accept Messiah-Christ as his Lord and Savior, and Jesus' death in substitution for our own, and cloaking man with the only sufficient justification and righteousness before God, and

Messiah-Christ's resurrection representing the first resurrection to be followed by the resurrection of all righteous men - first the dead, then followed by those alive - with admission to Life Eternal in Heaven.

Now, Where Are YOU Going?

Finally, let none of us be like the great Albert Einstein when he was on a train going to a station somewhere in New York. When the conductor came by and asked for his ticket, Albert could not find it. Einstein panicked, got down on his hands and knees, desperately searching. The conduc tor, at last recognizing the great Einstein, said, "Don't worry. I know who you are, Mr. Einstein, and I'm certain you bought a ticket, so there is no need to search further." Continuing to search desperately, Einstein replied, "Yes, I too know who _I am, but I must find my ticket, because *I don't know where I am going!*"[12]

Be certain to know where you are going! Secure your ticket (or passport) to Heaven - after all, it's a gift! We pray that Almighty God will inspire and bless your quest for peace, the true meaning of life and freedom, together with Eternal Salvation!

Also, Jo 1:1:

For one to persuade that all of this unimaginable variety - each unchanging with its own complicated intricacy, and design evolved over time from nothing would first need to prove that they are God! Regularity versus chance is itself instructive, the rising and setting of the sun daily, rather than once or twice a year or even a month is creative order by an omnipotent entity.

PART II

Reason for Our Hope:

Undeniable Proof of Our Creator God

CONTENTS

I.	Faith and Reason
II.	All of Nature with Its Incredible Magnificence, Provision, Regularity and Order
III.	Science
IV.	The Universe (& More Science)
V.	Archeological Findings – or Non-Findings-Wholly Supporting Scripture
VI.	The Truth that Scripture is God's Word – and that God's Word Is True!
VII.	Jesus, the Messiah/Christ: His Birth, Life, Crucifixion and Death
VIII.	The Bodily Resurrection of the Messiah – Jesus Christ
IX.	Jesus Christ – the ONLY person in all History who declared:
X.	Why a Messiah – Jesus Christ? – the "Legal" Issue
XI.	Deposits within each of us of a Free-Will and Creative mind Possessing a Self-consciousness, a Conscience and Innate Search for Meaning, Purpose, Right & Wrong, Plus a Dream Capacity
XII.	Evil: Its Origination, Place and End
XIII.	Total Inability of Any Human to Fully Comply with the Laws of Moses and the Ten Commandments Not a Single One of the Abrahamic Faithful nor Those Who Have Been Converted to Christ, despite Possessing the Indwelling Holy Spirit
XIV.	Worldwide Institutions of Caring – All Established Only as a Result of Jesus' Teachings of Love, Caring, Giving, Sacrifice Giving Rise to Christian Discipling and Witness
XV.	Revolutionary Changes in People Occurring Only as the Result of Their Conversion
XVI.	Daily God Experience/Communications/Dream/Directions/Strength/Comfort and Miracles
XVII.	Thousands of Near–Death Experiences of People – Allowed to Briefly Visit Christ Before Returning to the World
XVIII.	With a Sincere and Pure Heart, Ask God in Prayer to Reveal Himself to You!
XIX.	OK – It is Clear that God Created Us – But Just Who Created God??
XX.	Now, and Finally – How about YOU?

Reason for Our Hope
Undeniable Proof of Our Creator God

I. Faith And Reason

Beyond a superficial "belief," most folks dismiss or "postpone" seeking or receiving any true faith involving a willing obedience to God because 1) they don't want to change their current lifestyle, 2) they can't believe in a God who would allow "evil in the world", and /or 3) they rationalize that people of faith have acted blindly - ignoring all reason, intellect and "science."

In fact, God tells us that"... faith is being sure of what we hope for, and certain of what we do not see!" (Heb II:I), and to "always be prepared to give an answer to everyone who asks you to give the reasons for the hope that you have..." (I Peter 3:15)

> *"In the beginning was the Word, and the Word was with God and the Word was God."*
> Jo1:1(Word in Greek is "logos" - meaning "logic" or "reason.")

To help achieve our faith with reason, God has provided us with 66 Books, 40 authors and some 2,000 pages of scripture, along with true "scientific" facts, to study. By providing such a large amount of information and data, God is appealing to our minds, intellect and reason - not blind emotion, wishful thinking, or gut reaction.

In this connection also note the following related statements (that could only be made) by God:

> *"I will destroy the wisdom of the wise; the intelligence of the intelligent I will frustrate."* I Cor. 1:19
> *"The foolishness of God is wiser than man's wisdom, and the weakness of God is stronger than man's strength."* I Cor 1:25

Of course, to be sure there is a sense in which one's Faith in God- and His Messiah Son, Jesus-is "blind," and interpret nothing set forth in this writing as detracting from or adding to that sense.

Thus, the fundamental fact is that one's Faith if and when it comes is always and ultimately only the result of God's Grace." *...For it is by grace you have been saved, through haith...it is the gift of God - not by works so that no one can boast*" (Eph 2:8-9). This is all consistent with His having elected us, not our electing Him, despite the frequent appearance that we are doing so. Accordingly, one can know and accept all of the evidence in the world supporting the existence of our Creator-God and may even" believe" in the Creator-God like Satan and his demons, but still never receive God's gift of Faith.

> *"You believe that there is one God. You do well. (But) even the demons believe...and tremble!"* Jas 2:19

However, despite a world where Satan and sin have so much ill-effect, many folks possess minds open to reason and evidence and free of the frequent anti-creator bias of either the Scientist or Academic, retaining "soil" open to the "seed" of God's Grace and gift of Faith. It is these open minds we seek "to give reason."

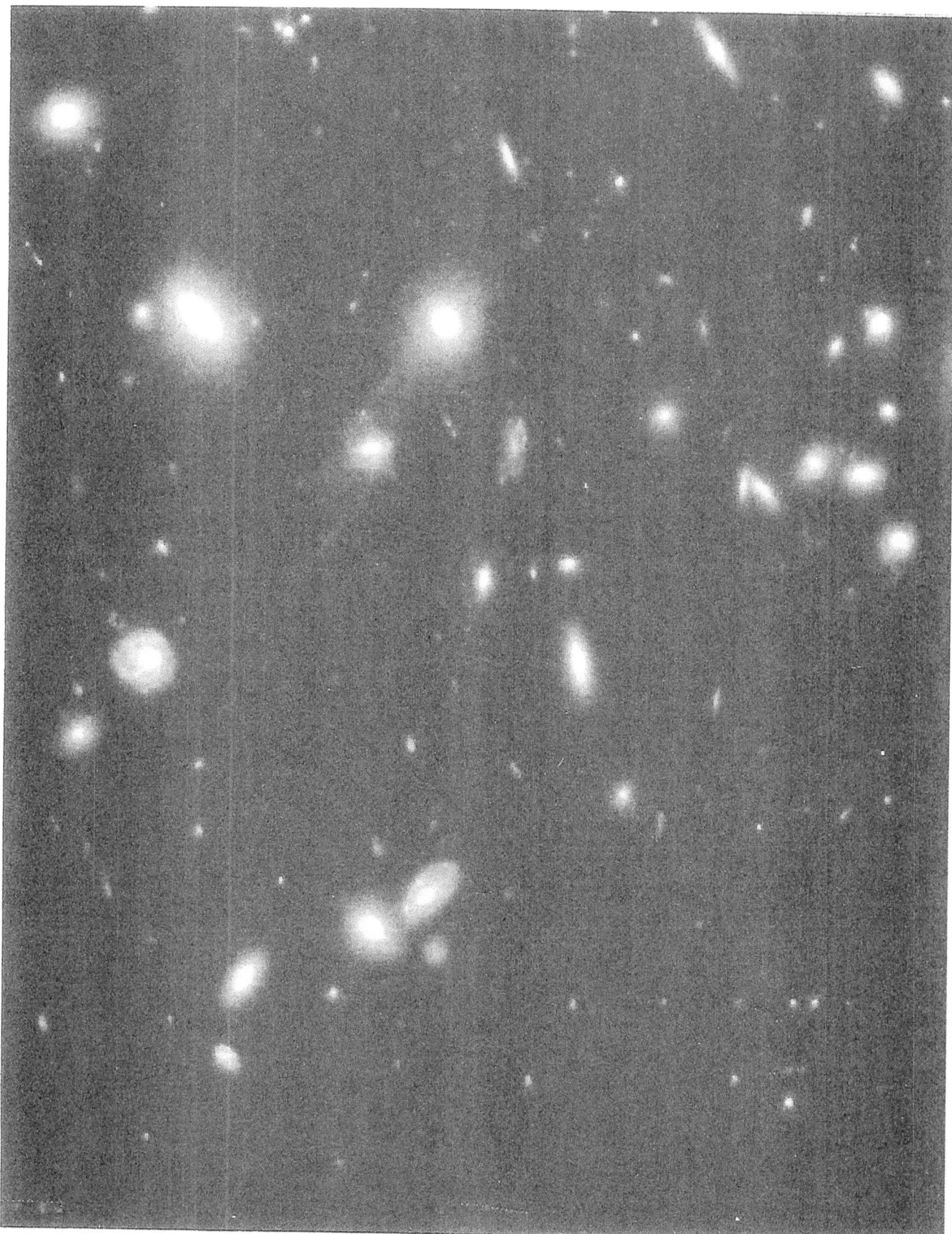

GALAXY CLUSTER is representative of what the universe looked like when it was 60 percent of its present age. The *Hubble Space Telescope* captured the image by focusing on the cluster as it completed 10 orbits. This image is one of the longest and clearest exposures ever produced. Several pairs of galaxies appear to be caught in one another's gravitational field. Such interactions are rarely found in nearby clusters and are evidence that the universe is evolving.

II.   All of Nature with Its Incredible Magnificence, Provision, Regularity and Order

- The earth being round, a globe or circular

- For nearly 3,000 years plus man and man's "science" considered the earth to be flat (The Egyptians thought it was supported by 6 huge pillars!). The Bible at Isaiah 40:22 states: "He (God) sits enthroned above the circle of the earth."{Other translations reference "sphere."}

- The "rising and setting" of the sun (see Part III, Science)

- The moon, some 400 billion planets, and trillions of stars (for the first 3,000 years men of science believed the stars to number 1026)

- The oceans with their salt and their critical tides tied to both sun and moon! The four seasons

- All varieties of trees, flowers, fruits, vegetables and grains Invaluable minerals throughout the earth

- The incredible variety and uniqueness of animals, birds and fish (over 20,000 varieties), including the miraculous:

- only the woodpecker's skull has been designed thick enough to sustain the harsh hammering of its bill without its fracturing;

- the tiny hummingbird's heart beats 1400 times per minute and has 4 chambers just like yours and mine!)

- a caterpillar's transformation into a butterfly

- 15,000species of mammals, each with 4 chambered hearts; if evolution, which of the 3 essentials of the cardio-vascular system along with oxygen came first - a beating heart, vessels, blood???

- Man with his two "non-evolvable," eyes (See Part III, Science)

- A Self-consciousness, a Conscience and creative nature with an innate seeking of life's meaning, purpose, etc.

- The Laws of nature and physics, with just the right positioning and amount of Sun,

- Law of Gravity

- Moon, vegetation, gravity, oxygen, carbon dioxide, neutrons, protons, salt and fresh water to sustain life

- Only recently discovered is the fact that our universe is currently expanding, which in reverse means it had a definite beginning -whether with or without a big bang! Thus, it is not an infinite universe, self-existent and constant. (See Part III, Science and Part IV, The Universe)

- God's Rainbow: *"I have set my rainbow in the clouds, and it will be the sign of the covenant between me and the earth...never again will the waters become a flood to destroy all life."* Gen. 9:13- 15

- *"What may be known about God is plain...God's invisible qualities - His external power and divine nature have been clearly seen being understood from what has been made, so that men are without excuse."* (Ro1:19- 20)

- See Genesis I for God's detailed account of creation, something only a God could create, or describe.

- *"By faith we understand that the universe was formed at God's command."* (Heb II:3)

III. Science

- See all of the above, including a flat vs. round earth.

- George Washington (along with many others) died as the results of having blood withdrawn from his body – on several occasion – during what proved to be his final illness. Blood removed from ill patients was common practice by placing outside their place of business the "red and the white striped poles" that we are all familiar with outside many barber shops yet today!

  Ignored by such "scientists" was God instruction for the past 3,000 years which would not only prohibit therapeutic blood draws - but would support today's practice of administering, not withdrawing, blood. "The *Life* of Every creature is its *Blood*!" (Lev. 17:14)

- 3,500-year-old OT Scripture teachings commanded circumstances to be done on the 8th day of life (Lev 12:3, Gen 17:8); medical science has only recently demonstrated to be done that blood coagulability is at its height- Yes, on the day of life!

- "As physician and scientist, I can finally attest to the attest to the fact that it is impossible for natural selection to explain the amazing intricacies of the eye" (let alone 2!) Ming Wang, M.D., PhD, world renowned eye surgeon and laser physicist at MIT

- Note Charles Darwin's Theory was "Origin of the Species": - not Life; Darwin wrote: "Science yet throws no light on the light on the far higher problems of the essence or origin of life"

- In the r940's, Anthony Flew, the world's then most notorious atheist presented his paper on Atheism at Oxford University's Socratic Club, chaired by C. S. Lewis. Thereafter, in 2004, at age 80, Flew wrote, "There is a God!" this conclusion following his investigation of DNA's enormous complexity which he acknowledged required a super intelligence. And, of course, C.S. Lewis himself later published his international classic "Mere Christianity" in 1943.

- What is more complicated: a jet plane, your iPhone, or a worm? All scientists agree it is

- the worm - by far!

- Self-creation of a single protein molecule - the most complicated substance known - is estimated at IO million to I, when in the field of logical, mathematical possibility, a ratio of 1050 to I is considered impossible.

- Despite many college textbooks stating that all scientists agree on Evolution:

  "There is no evidence, scientific or otherwise, to support the Theory of Evolution. " Sir Anthony Fleming of UK; Prof. Louis Agassiz, Harvard.

  Theodosius Dobzhansey, French scientist and world's leading Zoologist with "encyclopedic" knowledge, of whom it is stated that you may disagree - but you can't ignore him - and he "has demolished evolution on every front."

  Sir Julian Huxley: "I suppose many of us leaped at Darwin's work because the idea of God interfered with our sexual mores."

- Discovery of DNA in 1953 by James Watson and Francis Crick, later defined in detail by Francis Collins - so intricate, complicated, consistent and incredible that virtually all scientists now agree that only intelligent design could possibly explain DNA - never haphazard evolution.

  Note: Some have argued that in light of the genetic differences between man and ape being only 4%, this is evidence of evolution. However, it is the opposite that is true, since 4% makes total sense given the vast similarities between the two.

68

Further, a 4 % difference consists of 3 billion base pairs of DNA in every cell representing 120 million different entries in DNA codes -the equivalent of about 12 mil lion words! This is quite enough to explain the differences between ape and man.

4% also makes sense when you realize that roughly 1/1ooth of 1% accounts for all the differences between men - and man and woman -with this 1/10oth representing some 300,000 different code entries, or 30,000 words.

There is but one human race; In the beginning ALL were tan skin in color: after Tower of Babel – as people groups Narrowed some grew lighter and others darker in color.

Finally, would not a common designer (God) naturally and logically use a common DNA blueprint scheme for all living creatures - varying each just enough to create the Creator's desired result?

IV.   The Universe (& More Science)

- Not all that long ago, Galileo and subsequent scientists confirmed the fact that the earth revolves around the sun - not the reverse. Further, it has been observed that the sun itself is not stationary, and in fact travels at a speed of 600,000 mph as it moves through the vast space of the universe - a circuit so large that it would take (ca) 200 million years to complete one orbit. Wow, read that again! This is all consistent with scripture at Ps. 19:6: "Its (the sun's) rising is from one end of heaven and the circuit to the other end "- written some 4,000 years ago!

- Theories of Leading Physicists, Astro - physicists et al:

  Early on - from Aristotle to Galileo to Einstein to Sagan - all agreed that the universe was constant and had always existed - and that the "cosmos is all that is, ever was, or ever will be."

  Plato and Aristotle both sought to explain the cause of motion, since a universe at rest would be natural, but one in motion would be "unnatural."

  Sir Isaac Newton (1643-1727) who is entombed in Westminster Abby was perhaps the world's most renowned scientist. Newton spent the first half of his life on science; in particular, with his contributions on the quantification of universal gravitational attraction ("Principia"), white light's immutable spectral colors, optics including creation of one of the earliest telescopes, formulations of calculus, and alchemy (chemistry).

  Newton stated:

  > "Gravity explains the motions of the planets, but it
  > cannot explain who set the planets in motion. God governs
  > all things and knows all that is or can be done."

To the further chagrin of perhaps half of those scientists who publicly acknowledge being atheistic or agnostic, Newton spent much of the second half of his life in Theology, writing numerous Christian/religious works and teaching at both Trinity College and Cambridge University, fully accepting the resurrected Christ as son of God, though rejecting Trinitarian theology. Newton's research concluded that Christ's crucifixion occurred on 4/3/0 0 33.

The Universe (Continued)

After Sandage and Gunn and their Palomar telescope, and the early work of Slipher came Edwin Hubble and the Hubble telescope in 1929 - all in follow-up to Galileo's work in the 16oo's with their observations that the "farther away the stars, the redder they get" (the red shift effect)- leading to the certain conclusion that the universe with all of its galaxies is a constantly expanding one.

This was followed by Einstein's Theory of Relativity confirming an expanding universe and Einstein's confessing that he had previously "manipulated" a key number in order to keep from concluding an expanding universe which he had previously dismissed.

This led to the work of physicists Arvin Borde, Alexander Vilenkin, and Alan Guth- and the "BVG" theorems - concluding that any expanding universe had to have a beginning, indeed a very sudden beginning.

Fr. Georges LeMaitre, a Belgian physicist (and priest), when combining Einstein's theory of gravity which implied an expanding space, with the observation that galaxies were receding from each other, concluded that there had to have been a sudden "Big Bang" beginning.

Stephen Hawking joined in their opinions - supporting the universe's sudden beginning. All of these conclusions led to the work of Vilenkin, Roger Penrose and others regarding the theory of entropy and the second law of thermodynamics concluding that all stationary physical systems must necessarily run down and eventually die - perhaps by a firey death- as their energy dissipates. However, given a constantly expanding universe, and one with relatively low entropy at its beginning, the universe can continue on for a long time due to its continued expansion and ongoing energy source.

Physicist Hawking at least early on took the view that since "quarks" can occur and dis appear spontaneously, therefore, perhaps something could be created from nothing - including the Universe "given the laws of physics and nature." Of course, Hawking could never explain how or who it was that created these laws.

Regarding the scientific views of the age of the earth and its rocks, etc., know that it has been concluded that radioactive decay rates were greatly sped up at some point. Further, just when or how were the radiometric clocks set at the beginning?

Finally, there are the "fine-tuning" features of the universe. This includes the precise distances and angles of the sun and the moon, the force of gravity, the protons and neutrons, and the nuclear forces holding atom particles together where a 2% variance either way produces disaster - either no hydrogen with no life or all hydrogen and no life.

All of this has led to the following reluctant statements by the following, mostly agnostic scientists:

- "Only a super-calculating, super- intellect could cause or create the universe;"

and

- "At first sight one might think the strong anticlerical bias of modern science would be totally at odds with western religion. This is far from being so, how ever. The big bang theory requires a recent origin of the universe that openly invites the concept of creation, and where so-called thermodynamic theories of the origin of life in the organic soup of biology are the contemporary equivalent of the voice in the burning bush and the tablets of Moses."

Fred Hoyle Astronomer

- "If a watch proves the existence of a watchmaker but the universe does not prove the existence of a great architect, then I consent to be called a fool!"

Voltaire, Philosopher

- "The best data we have (relative to the "Big Bang") are exactly what I would have predicted had I nothing to go on but the books of Moses, the Psalms and the Bible as a whole."

Arno Panzias, Physicist, Nobel Laureate

- "Certain it is that a...rationality and intelligibility of the world lies behind all scientific work of a higher order...this firm belief...of a superior mind that reveals itself in the world of experience, represents my conception of God"

Einstein

- "The vast mysteries of the universe should only confirm our belief in the certainty of the Creator."
  "One cannot be exposed to the law and order of the universe without concluding that there must be design and purpose behind it all."

Wernher von Braun, Rocket Scientist

- UFO's and Possible "ET Life:'

  There is substantial evidence in support of these phenomena the existence of which we contend would be further evidence of a Creator-God. However, we would suggest that whatever "life" is involved is "soul-less" and/or the product of Evil and is being or will be used by God for His purposes which we will not fully understand until Eternity.

NOTE:

Know that "Science" is a billion of dollars industry supporting millions of "scientists" many of whom would be seen as losing their academic or scientific "objectivity" and quite possibly their positions if they professed/confessed publicly their belief in a Creator-God.

V. Archeological Findings – or Non-findings – Wholly Supporting Scripture

- The "Cambrian explosion" evidencing a sudden explosion; "All major groups of invertebrates appear suddenly in the very first fossiliferous (Cambrian) strata," Prof. Enoch, Zoologist, University of Madras.

- Signs of a World-wide Flood (which killed all who did not heed God's warning). Desiring none to perish, God is once again warning the world - not of flood, but fire.

- Convincing evidence and remnants of large numbers of Jews having lived in Egypt between 1500 and1200 B.C.

- Evidence of the Exodus and Red Sea Crossing (ca) 1275

- Uncovering physical evidence of many old Biblical names and places

- Finding both OT and NT Scripture writings -with many authentic document fragments as old as 1000+ years B.C., including the Dead Sea Scrolls - See Part VI

- Finding physical remnants of many OT/NT sites in Jerusalem and Israel

- It is highly significant that no meaningful transitional links, nor even a single transitional vertebrate, have ever been found despite the vast number of archeological dig sites throughout the world - an impossibility with any macro- evolutionary process

- ALL 4 Anchors of Paul's ship that was wrecked off Malta have been found – in 90 feet of water [See Act 27]

- While the Shroud of Turin could alone present strong evidence of Christ's existence and resurrection given its mysterious "negative" photographic image, early "Carbon 14" dating analyses placed the shroud at (ca) 1000 AD, although given recent ad

- Voltaire predicted that IO0 years after his death (in 1728) the Bible would disappear. Instead, 50 years after his death - in 1778 - Voltaire 's home was being used by the Geneva Bible Society to print Bibles! (God surely has a sense of irony and humor!)

- The Israeli Nation ceased to exist after 70 AD and was absent from the world scene for some 2000 years with its peoples dispersed throughout the world. However, Isaiah, at II:12, in 200 BC or so prophesied:

"He will gather the exiles of Israel - the scattered people of Judah from the four quarters of the earth;" and Amos at 9:14 prophesied: "I will bring back my exiled people Israel I will plant Israel in their beloved land - never again to be uprooted from the land I have given them, says the Lord, your God."

- In May 1948, Israel was recognized by the U.S. and U.N. as a Nation re-born to its former and present location. Further, in 1967 Jerusalem was returned to Israel. (If the Israeli Nation should ever again cease to exist - or Jerusalem leave Israeli control - God will have been wrong - an impossibility!)

- Tyre - a prominent Phoenician Mediterranean city was destroyed, and OT scripture at Ez. 28:19 promised - "will never again arise." The city has not - and never will!

- "The lamb at the center of the throne will be their shepherd; he will lead them to springs of living water." (Rev 7:17) "Whoever believes in me, as the scripture has said, streams of living water will flow from within Him." (Jo 7:38) "On that day living water will flow out from Jerusalem." (Zech 14:8)

- For the 2000 years that the Israelites were dispersed the lands of Canaan lay mostly arid. "Miraculously" over the years since the return of Israel to its lands, streams of water have begun to appear throughout the land providing Israel with 10 times its original water supply - allowing Israel to provide both fresh water and an abundance of fruits and vegetables to both its people and those of neighboring lands, including the Palestinians.

- Prophecies regarding the fast approaching "end times" (see Matt 24; 2 Peter, et al.)

  o increasing hostilities, particularly among nations in and around the Mid-East; increasing earthquakes, famines and other life-threatening events;

  o disbelief of Noah's flood;

  o growing empty/dead /non-gospel preaching churches; worldwide Christian persecutions;

  o seeking of worldwide rule - but not God (Babel)

  o 24/7 cable news and "smart" phones;

  o 24/7 sexual immorality and lust (Babylon);

  o increasing fears (fear of God only casteth out all other fears}; disrespect for life, sexual identity and traditional family units;

  o boastful self-pride, lovers of self - not God; (all in total denial of the fact that whatever good we have or do comes only from God!).

  o Note: Recent polls of people who even say they are Christian reflect a decline from 90% to 65+%, while authentic Christianity is perhaps IO%. Our understanding of the variability in atmospheric C-14 the date could be much earlier. However, a 1994 publication by Pickney and Prince provides credible evidence that the shroud was likely "created" by the eccentric genius Leonardo DaVinci in the late 1400's

- REGARDING BABEL, AND THE WORLD'S DIFFERENT LANGUAGES

Have you ever thought how the vastly different languages of peoples and nations originated- Chinese, Russian, Greek, Arabic, English, etc. These languages were, and could only have been created by God, and for his purposes.

Just as deceived people lacking in wisdom today seek total rule by their government, and ultimately by a world government, so did the people over the years following the Flood, at a time when the world's smaller population had only one language and a common speech. These people become egotistical, full of self-pride, and decided to build a tower (Babel) "so they might reach into God's Heaven."

Seeing the evil this would bring, God confused their language so that they could not understand one another. As a result, each of the various language groups were forced to separate themselves from one another becoming scattered over the earth. (See the Word of God at Gen 11:1-9)

Also, note pre-historic stone structures and building techniques that exist yet today on all continents evidence of dispersion of the people, and with the people their common skills learned prior to Babel.

Vi.   The Truth that Scripture is God's Word- and that God's Word Is True! All Prophecies proven 100% Accurate

- 66 books of both Old and New Testament books – some 2,000 pages written over a period of some 1,600 years by 40 different scribes speaking in 3 different languages: Hebrew, Greek and Aramaic.

- All 66 Books interrelate with many intertwining references- a total impossibility without an overarching God, inspiring and directing each and all of the 40 different scribes working in different languages.

- Scripture describes people/events/sites that have been evidenced by numerous archeological findings and historians' writings.

- Scripture – The Old Testament contains some 300 specific prophecies of the Messiah – some 60 or so pertaining the birth of Christ – every single one providing true. There are hundreds of other prophesies in both the OT and NT also proven 100% true to date, with many events yet to occur. Not a single prophecy has been wrong. The chance of predicting "just 8 of these predictions all being correct would be the same as blind man picking a single mark silver dollar out of silver dollars stacked 2' high across the entire State of Texas- according to mathematician Peter Stone in "Science Speaks" See Part VII, Ps. 22 and Isaiah 53 for just a few examples of compelling and totally convincing prophecies.

- John's Gospel written (ca) 60 AD quotes 153 fish caught in an unbroken net as John and Jesus – post resurrection – watched as eye – witnesses. Why an unbroken net? Because Jesus was prophesying that men from every nation would be "caught", and not lost on "His" net. Why 153? Only Jesus could know that the yet unborn Oppian would go on to then know write in about 200 AD "Oppian's Catalogue of Fishes" recording that the variety of all then known fish was numbers at – 153!

- Note again the reference in Part III above re: 8th day circumcision and medical science's recent confirmation…

- Scripture's continuity, harmony, inter-related verses among 40 authors speaking 3 different languages over a 1600 – year period 2000 to 3000 years ago.

- Early Scripture Survival: Despite continuing attacks by Satan and opponents over more than 3000 years, including burning both books and martyrs at the stake, both before and after the first printing press copies in 1458. Remarkably, as of about 150 AD, the following number of hand-written copies existed: Julius Caesar: 10; Homer's Iliad: 600; Bible: 24,000

- GOD's dispersion of the people from the tower of Babel explains the widely different languages of peoples.

- Bibles today: over a billion copies of the Bible have been printed in 24,000 languages, far more than any book in history.

- Dead sea scrolls: Discovered in a cave in the 1940's dating (ca) 400 BC proved to be identical to current copies of OT books.

Read just a few of the thousands of excerpts from Scripture cited below and convince yourself that anyone of them could possibly have been inspired by man - rather than God, encompassing His enduring Truths!

"In the beginning was the Word...and the Word was God...through Him all things were made." (Jo1:1-3)

"I will put enmity between you and the woman and between your offspring and hers - he will crush your head and you will strike his heel" (Gen. 3:15)

"Before I formed you in the womb, I knew you." (Jeremiah 1"5)

"...except a man be born again he cannot see the Kingdom of God." (John 3:3)

"It is easier for a camel to go through the eye of a needle than for a rich man to enter the Kingdom of GOD" [Mt 19:24]

"For I have come to turn a man against his father, a daughter against her mother..." (Ma tt. 10:35)

"Blessed are the meek, for they shall inherit the earth." (Matt.5:5)

"Love your enemies...pray for them who persecute you." (Matt 5:44)

"The stone the builders rejected has become the capstone."(Ps.IIB:22)

"The stone the builders rejected has become the capstone."(Ps.IIB:22)

"The kingdom of heaven is like a man who finds treasure hidden in a field and sells all he has and buys the field." (Matt 13:44)

"...Destroy this temple, and in three days I will raise it up..." (John 2:19)

"Take my yoke upon and learn from me, for I am gentle and humble in heart, and you will find rest for your souls." [Matt 11:58]

VII.   Jesus, the Messiah/Christ: His Birth, Life, Crucifixion and Death

- Well-known non-Christians living in Jesus' time have each written of Jesus' existence and life - some referencing His alleged resurrection; following are just a few:

  - <u>Pliny</u> the Younger, Roman Governor, (n2 AD) Tacitus, Historian (II2 AD)

  - <u>Josephus</u>, Jewish Historian (90 AD), - including describing an earthquake in (ca) 31 AD (at Jesus' crucifixion?)

  - <u>Thallus</u>, Historian - who wrote of the blacking out of the sun on the day of Jesus' crucifixion

  - <u>Suetonius</u>, Roman archivist

- Following are a few of the nearly 500 Old Testament Prophesies written at least some 700 plus years earlier - describing specific details of the birth, betrayal, suffering, crucifixion, death and sacrificial lamb of Jesus:

Genesis 3:15
"You (Satan) will strike his heel"
Micah 5:2:
"But you, Bethlehem Ephrathah, though you are small among the clans of Judah, out of you will come for me one who will be ruler over Israel whose origins are from of old, from ancient times."
Zechariah 11:12-13:
"Throw it to the potter - the 30 pieces of silver...the handsome price at which they priced me!"
Psalm 22:
"My God, my God, why have you forsaken me?" "They have pierced my hands and feet."
"I can count all my bones."
"They divide my garments and cast lots for my clothing."
Psalm 41:9:

"Even my close friend whom I trusted...has lifted up his heel against me."

<u>Isaiah 53:</u>

"He was pierced for our transgressions, crushed for our iniquities;" "by his wounds we are healed."

"...the Lord has laid on Him the iniquity of us all."

"He was led like a lamb to the slaughter, and as a sheep before her shearers is silent, so He did not open his mouth."

VIII. The Bodily Resurrection of the Messiah - Jesus Christ

For totally convincing evidence of the central/critical event in history - namely the Bodily Resurrection of Jesus after His crucifixion and death - See Part I of this book, "Resurrection: Fact or Fiction, A Trial Lawyer Looks at All of the Evidence."

•   An Abbreviated Summary of Primary Evidence of Jesus' Resurrection:

Jesus was crucified; Jesus died on the Cross with a sword having been plunged into His side; Jesus was buried in a specific, well-known tomb; the apostles immediately went into despair; Jesus initially appeared (in bodily form) to 3 women (at the time considered to be unreliable as witnesses); Matthew, Peter, John, Paul and James, Jesus' brother, Served as both eyewitnesses and New Testament authors; all of the apostles-including doubting Thomas, who placed his hand in Jesus' side; 500 people at one time, and finally to Paul on the Damascus Road; the tomb was empty; Jesus appeared in Jerusalem - where His body could have been easily produced by His opponents; Jewish converts changed their Holy Day from Saturday to Sunday; early on celebration of the sacraments and Easter; early artwork and hymns; the apostles were transformed from total despair to preaching the Gospel, and all of the apostles (except John)were martyred for their belief rather than denying Jesus' resurrection, and in succeeding years thousands have given their lives for their belief in a resurrected Christ, none more notable than Polycarp in about the year 120 A.D. James - Brother of Jesus - "overnight" converted from family Skeptic to Believer; Paul was converted from Saul, the Chief Prosecutor of Jesus to Chief Evangelist for Jesus upon the appearance and revelation of Christ to Saul; "Christian Church's" sudden growth throughout the world with the cross becoming the world's most recognizable symbol ever; the central Gospel message of Bodily Resurrection was taught within months of the Resurrection; within IO to 20 years most of the NT scriptures appeared (led by James, Galatians, I Corinthians, I Thessalonians); some 500 prophesies of Messiah in OT have all come true; all blood sacrifices ended shortly after Jesus' Resurrection; the appearance of Messiah roughly mid-way in human history - (before cable news!) - all in God's perfect timing; note miraculous workings of the Holy Spirit transforming lives throughout history and every day - as well as miracles of God every day.

IX.   Jesus Christ -the ONLY person in all of History who declared:

"I am the way, the truth and the Life;" (Jo. 14:6)

"I and the Father (God) are one!" (Jo. II:30)

"I am the resurrection and the life. He who believes in me...will never die." (Jo. II:25)

"I give them (my sheep) eternal life, and they shall never perish." (Jo. II:28)

Additionally, the voices of God: "This is my Son, whom I have chosen, listen to him" (Luke9:35)

"You are my Beloved son, with you I am well pleased." (MK. 1::11)

As such, Jesus was either Liar, Lunatic or Lord! - You choose but know that your Eternal destiny rests on the Answer!

X.   Why a Messiah - Jesus Christ? - the "Legal" Issue

Jesus Christ, our Savior - is also our Counselor. He came to the world to deal with the legal consequences for each of us - and all humanity - whereby having broken God's law by sinning, we are guilty as charged before God.

However, being both our legal Counselor and Mediator - as Son of God, and God - Jesus pleads before God the Father and Judge: "I will pay the penalty" - the penalty being His substitutionary death for us and our sin.

All that is required is for each sinner to repent and retain/request Jesus to represent him/her before God's Holy Tribunal having accepted Jesus' penalty of death as our own!

XI.   Deposits within each of us of a Free-Will and Creative Mind Possessing a Self-consciousness, a Conscience and Innate Search for Meaning, Purpose, Right & Wrong, Plus a Dream Capacity

Each of the above could only be God-created, being totally incapable of any evolutionary process. Indeed, with God telling us that we have been "created in His image," it is these features that are most significant, and explain mankind's unique capacities for creativity, search for meaning and purpose, caring, empathy, compassion, God's agape' love, and quest for life eternal.

XII.   Evil: Its Origination, Place and End

God did not create Evil and hates it. He arranged for Messiah to come and conquer it, and He provides armor for His children to combat it - and, in the next world He will ban it - with Satan and his followers being assigned to the lake of Eternal Fire.

However, our loving God created both the angels and man with a Free Will. Lucifer, like many human creations to follow, defied God, becoming Satan and was followed by a third of the angels - now demons. All were promptly expelled from heaven and relegated to the world. Be assured that while the absence of Satan and Evil is God's plan for Heaven - He is allowing Satan to serve His purposes in in our current world. Given our human natures God in His mercy knows that many turn to Him only in the desperation of our sufferings -rarely in the delight of our blessings. God also wants us to see how vulnerable life is in an evil world. As such God wants us to deal with the question of our Eternal Life today - not tomorrow!

Having gifted us with Free Will God wants each of us to seek Jesus as Counselor, Lord and Savior - doing so in a deliberate exercise of our Free Will. God intends the world to be a meaningful experience and challenge and to prove the worthiness and genuine ness of those seeking admission to Life Eternal. Without the presence of the evil spirits of Satan and his demons - the world would present insufficient adversity, challenge and testing for most of us to evidence the genuine exercise of our Free Wills and the granting of God's Grace and gift of Faith.

Remember, even Jesus was tempted by Satan while Jesus was in the world. Further, Jesus did not question Satan's statement: "I will give you all authority of the kingdoms of the world, for it has been given to me...if you worship me, it will be yours." Jesus' answer should be ours: "It is written: 'Worship the Lord your God and serve Him only.'" (Luke 4:5-8)

Additionally, God is pure, Holy and true. He and we know the difference between true and meaningful love and caring for others, as opposed to the cheap, and false expressions of caring for others such as we see among those who promote a highly superficial "politically correctness." Only the indwelling Holy Spirit and God's love can motivate one's true and boundless love and caring for all.

God warns us that it is the Spiritual World and that which is unseen - including our souls and the Holy Spirit - which are most important - not the seen and physical, nor the flesh and blood of the physical world. The Holy Spirit is critical to both our conversion, and protection from evil as we pass through the world. In opposition, there are the spiritual demons and Satan who God is allowing -for a time -to reign as Prince of the Air - though always subject to God's ultimate authority. Note well, however, that despite the pervasiveness of evil in the world, God's love in the world still overcomes. This is the result of the work of God's children and Jesus' disciples, aided by the armor of God (Ephes 6:13), the spreading of salt and light and the Holy Spirit, all enabling God's goodness and Will to prevail.

In this further connection, note well God's promise at Ro.8:28":..in ALL *things God works for the good of those who love Him, who have been called according to His purpose."*

XIII. Total Inability of Any Human to Fully Comply with the Laws of Moses and the Ten Commandments Not a Single One of the Abrahamic Faithful nor Those Who Have Been Converted to Christ, despite Possessing the Indwelling Holy Spirit

"...all of our righteous acts are like filthy rags." (Is. 64:6)
"...there is no one righteous, not even one..."(Ro: 3:10)

XIV. Worldwide Institutions of Caring - All Established Only as a Result of Jesus' Teachings of Love, Caring, Giving, Sacrifice Giving Rise to Christian Discipling and Witness

- Life for all, including children and those in the womb. "Before I formed you in the womb I knew you, before you were born, I set you apart." (Jere 1:5) "Better for him if a mill stone were hung around his neck and he were thrown into the depths of the sea than he should offend one of these little ones." (Luke u:2) Note: In Greco-Roman and many other eras, infants were often sacrificed.

- Opposition to Old Testament "slavery" - Note: Author of "Real Christianity" - William Wilberforce conducted a 25-year peaceful campaign initiated by John Newton and John Wesley resulting in banning slavery in the UK in 1835, an effort followed by America 's painful Civil War, 1861-1865, largely initiated by Christian abolitionists.

- Health Care - the first hospitals throughout the world were initiated by Christian churches, groups and organizations.

- Education: Thanks to Guttenberg's printing press in 1458, followed by the Protestant Reformation, Bibles were put into the hands of the common people, with public schools being instituted for the specific purpose of teaching the Bible, initially the only text book; the first universities ("one out of diversity") were begun by Christians; however, most of today's universities, including Harvard, et al. have long abandoned their early "Christian Charters" calling for teaching truth and reason, and the spread of salt and light.

- Charity: Whether through Christian churches, or institutions such as "The Red Cross," the Salvation Army, Good Will, YMCA, and many others, the fundamental concepts of charity were created by the Messiah Christ and His teachings, including "It is more blessed to give than to receive" (Acts 20:35), "Love thy neighbor as thyself"(Matt 22:39), and "Bring the whole tithe into the storehouse...test me in this...I will pour out so much blessing..."(Micah 3:10).

- Equality of all, including the dignity of women: Christ taught "There is neither Jew nor Greek, slave nor free, male nor female, (black nor white, etc.) - for you are all one in Christ Jesus." (Gal 31:28) Contrast this with -
Plato, who taught that cowardly men would be reincarnated as women, and
Aristotle, who taught that women fell somewhere between slave and free!

XV. Revolutionary Changes in People Occurring Only as the Result of Their Conversion

In addition to the many you know whose Faith is in our Lord, note below just a few well known examples of Christian conversions among the many millions producing total change in character and purpose - as well as destiny:

Saul, Chief Prosecutor of Jesus, meets the resurrected Jesus, is converted to "Paul," becoming Chief Apostle, Epistle writer, and Martyr

James, unbelieving brother of Jesus, converts, becoming leader of the Christian Church in Jerusalem, and eventual Martyr

All of the martyrs who have willingly given their very lives for their belief in God and the Resurrected Messiah, starting with Stephen, all of the Apostles (except John), Jesus' brother James, Paul, Polycarp, and thousands of others

Simon Greenleaf, Professor of Evidence, Harvard Law School, 1833-1848, author of "Testimony of the Evangelists," a skeptic who converted after studying all of the evidence; (Open-minded, take note!)

Stan Telchin, Jewish convert who authored "Betrayed," published in 1925;

C.S. Lewis, brilliant British professor and atheist who converted to Christianity after much study, writing "Mere Christianity" in 1943

Albert DiSalvo, "the Boston Strangler," 1962, converted while in prison, leading many convicts to Christ

Kris Kristofferson of Country Music fame whose parents had rejected his career, con verted while attending a church service at the invitation of a friend, leading him and others to compose many evangelistic songs

Chuck Colson, Watergate convict and agnostic, converted becoming an evangelist, and authored "Born Again".

Lee Strobel, atheist and journalist, who after thorough investigation converted and authored "Case for Christ," "Case for Faith," "Case for a Creator"(1998), etc., et al., et al.

XVI. Daily God Experiences/Communications /Dreams/ Directions/Strength/Comfort and Miracles

While perhaps not as dramatic as some of the Bible miracles, these events occur in the daily lives of His children - and often need only be recognized as God's interactions with us, instead of being dismissed as mere coincidence or chance!

XVII. Thousands of Near-Death Experiences of People - Allowed to Briefly Visit Christ Before Returning to the World

These folks provide many highly credible eye-witness accounts of their dramatic experiences of meeting Christ, deceased loved ones or other persuasive reports.

XVIII. With a Sincere and Pure Heart, Ask God in Prayer to Reveal Himself to You!

If you do, He will!

XIX. OK - It is Clear that God Created Us- But Just Who Created God??

Bertrand Russell, an atheist (who once stated he preferred atheism since he would not need to alter his amoral behavior):

> "I may say that when I was a young man and was debating these questions very seriously in my mind, I for a long time accepted the argument of the First Cause , until one day, at the age of eighteen , I read John Stuart Mills' autobiography, and I there found the sentence: "

> My father taught me that the question 'Who made me?' cannot be answered, since it immediately suggests the further question 'Who made God?'" That very simple sentence showed me, as I still think, the fallacy in the argument of the First Cause. If everything must have a cause, then God must have a cause. If there can be anything without a cause, it may just as well be the world as God."

This question has occurred to many of us. However, we must never be deceived by Satan's deceits including "everything has to have a cause." Once recognizing that God

- being Spirit - is the designer of all and created each of us with a spiritual component for a world in which the Spirit and unseen are most critical - we need be open to the logical conclusion that such an all-powerful Spiritual Designer is indeed and must be an uncaused Creator.

As scripture tells us:

> *"God... (with the Son) ...made the Universe." (Heb I:I-2)*

> *"In the beginning was the Word (and Spirit) ...and the Word was with God and the Word was God" (Jo 1:1). Also, "I am who I am." (Ex 3:14).*

XX. NOW, and Finally - How about YOU?

Remember, believing that there is a Creator God gives you at most only an <u>Undergraduate Degree</u> - merely <u>qualifying</u> you for your <u>Graduate Degree</u>. Even Satan and the demons hold undergraduate degrees - my, oh my, do they ever! However, as with <u>Nicodemus</u>, a member of the Sanhedrin who - after inquiring of Jesus, "What must I do to inherit Eternal life?" - Jesus answered: "<u>No one can see the Kingdom of God unless he is born again</u>" (Jn 3:3). There are also many folks, who, like the rich young man, when asking this same question, must first do as Jesus responded, "Sell all your possessions and give to the poor"(Matt 19). Thus, <u>to secure our Graduate Degree</u> and our Passport to Heaven, we must also <u>repent, believe in, accept, love and obey the Resurrected Christ and Son of God, accepting Him as our personal Savior and Counsellor,</u> putting on His cloak of righteousness thereby becoming <u>justified</u> in the sight of Holy God, and giving thanks <u>for His gift of Grace and Faith</u>, evidenced by the Holy Spirit residing in our regenerated hearts. As a result, God's love will flow from us like water over a waterfall motivating us to seek <u>obedience to His Will, follow His plan for our lives, and evidence sincere love</u> towards all!

Incidental to our Graduate Degrees, Christ also commissions each of us to "go and make disciples of all nations...teaching them to obey everything I have commanded... (knowing) I am with you always..."

(Matt. 28 :19- 20). Pray each day to recognize and seize every <u>opportunity</u>, including with every person you meet, to reflect in both words and acts the <u>Lord</u>, His <u>Word</u>, and His <u>Love</u>![1]

Even if we think we do nothing wrong or bad - we do - be it self-pride, not loving all others, not keeping the Sabbath Holy, nor putting God first and/or having no idols (e.g., spouse? children? sports? work?), along with our lies, covetousness, etc.

As such, we all stand convicted, and in need of repentance, redemption, justification and salvation through God's grace and gift of faith.

PART III

LIFE'S REALITY PLAY

ACT I: Life in This World
ACT II: A New World King
ACT III: Purely Elective

I. CONTENT

I.   **Life's Reality Play-An Outline of Life's and the Play's Major Events and Timetable**

   Act I Scene 1: Creation; Garden of Eden; Satan; Noah and the Flood (4000 to 2300 BC)

   Scene 2: Japheth, Ham & Shem, Abraham, Ishmael & Isaac; the near Sacrifice of Isaac; Joseph; Moses; the Exodus (2300 BC to 1000 BC)

   Scene 3: Israel; the Messiah's Birth, Life, Crucifixion and Resurrection; the Holy Spirit's appearing; the writings of the New Testament; destruction of the temple and Jerusalem (1000 BC to 70 AD)

   Scene 4: World Conflict among people and religions; Evil v. God; Spread of the Gospel message and God's Plan for mankind throughout the World (70 AD to 2040 AD)

   Scene 5: The "Last Days," Trials & Tribulations[1], the Rapture[2] and God's saving "Israel"[3] with fire (2040 to 2047 AD)

   Act II   Return of Messiah, 1000 year Reign of Christ, God's Critique of all Stage Actors and The Final Judgement

   Act III   Heaven on Earth Renewed (lasting for all Eternity!)

II.   Preface & Brief Overview of God's Plan and Life's Reality Play

III.   Observations of Play, Acts and Scenes

   A)   Overall Play
   B)   Observations Act I, Sc I
   C)   Observations Act I, Sc 2
   D)   Observations Act I, Sc 3
   E)   Observations Act I, Sc 4 Warnings against Being "of the World"
   •   The Mission of Christians
   •   Christian Engagement in the World
   •   Voting
   •   But is Not America - A Christian Nation?
   •   Salt, Light and Salvation Is Messiah Christ's Plan
   •   The Twin and Supports

82

F.) Observation of Act I, Sc 5

G.) Observation of Act II

H.) Observation of Act III

IV.   God's Play Lasts Thousands of Years - Why So Long?

V.   God is a Loving God!

VI.   God Hates Evil!

VII.   Why Does God Allow Any Evil in Act I - even if Good Outweighs all the Bad? Why Did God Create Lucifer/ Sat an in the First Place?

VIII. Insights into God's Conversion Process

IX.   Israel and America

X.   Two Final Notes

    • What Triggered this Book?

    • Who is the Audience in God's "Life's Reality Play?"

II. PREFACE

HOW CAN WE UNDERSTAND SUCH THINGS ASTHE HORRENDOUS HOLOCAUST, A MOTHER OR FATHER FACING THE TRAGIC DEATH OF THEIR CHILD, A SERIOUS ILLNESS OF A LOVED ONE, ANY INNOCENT PERSON WHO SUFFERS? AN ACT OF "NATURE" THAT KILLS MANY?

- IF LIFE IS GOD'S REALITY PLAY, WHAT SCENE IS NOW PLAYING?
- WHY IS THERE EVIL IN TODAY'S WORLD?
- GOD'S RESPONSE TO THOSE WHO SUFFER LOSS?
- ARE GOD'S PROMISES AND LOVE SURE?
- CAN GOD PREVENT EVIL FROM HAPPENING? IS GOD REALLY OMNIPOTENT?
- IF GOD CAN STOP EVIL, WHY DOES HE NOT? IS HE NOT A LOVING GOD?
- HOW CAN/WHY SHOULD WE GO ON LOVING OR BELIEVING IN A GOD WHO CAN, BUT DOES NOT ALWAYS ACTTO STOP EVIL?
- WHAT IS GOD'S PLAN FOR MANKIND?

A Brief Overview of God's Plan and Life's Reality Play

To begin to respond to the above, we must first see and gain some understanding of the "big picture" - an overview of God's Plan for humankind over all of World History including the future a period that will encompass perhaps 5,000 years or more. We must have perspective and ability to appreciate the time and place in which we who are currently alive and on life's stage find ourselves.

A helpful way to visualize all of this is to see God's Plan as a Life Reality Play - presented on the world stage. The Play that started maybe 5,000 years ago, and still has maybe 40 to 1,000 years, more or less, to go before the final Act commences.

It is also vital to understand that God is the playwright, having written the entire play of life - here presented in 3 Acts, with Act I consist of 5 scenes. God himself has set all the scenes, created all the actors, and at times appears and speaks Himself - sometimes "in person," sometimes as just a voice or in disguise. At times He speaks through others whose hearts He has renewed and/or whom He has inspired. On occasion, God takes direct action, including through "nature's forces" that He alone controls, be it flood, fire or some other force. Further, while God knows all that will happen or be said, for the most part God does not write the scripts of the various actors, leaving those to be spoken by each actor, though often times inspired by God.

Importantly, we need to understand that each of us now alive - are currently actors on the world stage appearing in Act I, Scene 4 - now underway. As such, we can and often do by our actions and words influence what does or is yet to occur on stage, perhaps unknown to us, but known to God. Some of us may go on to appear in Scene 5, a Scene that will be both brief and violent, and which will be detailed further below. Finally, a number of actors who have appeared in Act I, will reappear in Act III, but with new resurrected and indestructible bodies. Sadly, however, many of the World's actors will not appear in Act III. The good news is that you can appear, but to do so you need to know how - or - "the way!"

Finally, we need to refrain from thinking that this is all just "make-believe "or maybe true, maybe not. Whether conscious of it or not, we really do live our lives on the world stage, and as such we are always on camera though sometimes only "candid camera."[4]

---

4.   All the World's a stage and all men and women merely players - they have their entrances and exits..."
(Shakespeare's "As You Like It" Act II, Scene 7.)

III. OBSERVATIONS OF ACTS AND SCENES

A. Observations of the Overall Play

We know that God created both angels and men – many with great intelligence (though not always wisdom) and for reasons presented later – also created us with free wills, wills that often appear too strong and independent.

As a result, from the very earliest of times and consistently throughout History, we see many instances where – an angel (in the case of lucifer) – or a man (in the case of Hitler) – thinks he is God, wants to be God and/ or acts as or plays God. As such, these rebels seek to write their own version of life's play. On far lesser scales there are many on the World Stage today who thinks or act as if there is no God, and really thinks that he or she can be in control.

To avoid falling prey to nay such thinking here we should seek to understand but never questioning or criticizing God's plan or his Wisdom.

Hopefully, simply by seeing God's Plan-laid out here in his Reality Paly – we can begin to visualize, if not fully appreciate God's wisdom and purposes, and His over-arching plan for the development of human-kind and for the preparation of ma's soul for God's Final Act., His eternal kingdom. In doing so, our hope will be to gain some insights into the answer to the critical questions set forth in the Preface to this "Play Bool"

B. Observations of Act I, Scene 1

Act I, Scene I forms the World-stage, the initial actors and the Garden of Eden. Also appearing is the beautiful Angel Lucifer - now Satan - who along with one-third of his Angel-followers, have been ejected by God from Heaven and fallen into the World as devil and demons. Operating under his alias, Satan's initial earthly role was as the deceiving Serpent appearing to Eve and Adam. God having made man free and with very strong free wills enabled man to disobey God and chose to believe the Serpent's lie. (So too, we are all free to do so today.) As a result, God banned man from Eden but allowed Satan to assume the role of Earth's ruling Prince - the Prince of the Air. One might suggest that this was a bit like God saying to men, "OK, you made your bed, now go lay in it." However, in fact, Satan's protagonistic role as ruling Prince, will be allowed by Playwright God to continue throughout virtually all of Act I, but always with certain restraints. Further, in Scene 3 God will loosen the Holy Spirit who came to us at Jesus' Ascension, and arm all of God's children with the Armor of God enabling the defeat of Satan. Scene I ended with the Flood, destroying all of the rampant evil in the World but with a physical saving of the righteous Noah and his family-including Noah's 3 sons, Japheth, Ham and Shem.

At first glance, the Garden of Eden may seem a bit like it was God's Plan W - with God "thinking/hoping" that His real life drama could be a one Act Play, sort of Garden of Eden and Heaven being rolled into one.

This is a tempting hypothesis, since after man's fall, and 2,000 years or so of unspeakable evil, God drowns out the entire human race - all except Noah, who was a righteous man, along with Noah's family. As such, one might be tempted to argue that the flood was God's "admission" of having made a mistake, with God seeking to wipe the slate clean and try again. However, perish the thought!

Know well that God is omniscient, omnipotent, wise and patient! God is never surprised, never makes mistakes and none of His plans fail! God knows precisely what will happen and allows it to happen - not for His benefit - but for ours, and for our deeper understanding of the nature of God, man, and God's Plan. So, it was - and is - with the Flood, filled with God's lessons to mankind.

Note that in this day of some folks thinking that they can control the environment (despite being unable to even control themselves) it is interesting to note that it was God who initiated the first recorded environmental disaster - namely rain to come to Earth, last for 40 days, creating the Great Flood. At the end of the rain, God created the rainbow as the sign of His Covenant, prophetically promising never again to destroy the World's mankind by flood. Note at the end of Scene 5, Act I when prophesy seems to tell us that God will bring destruction to the enemy forces attacking "Israel," God will do so by sending fire down from above, not rain or flood waters. [5]

C. Observation Of Act I, Scene 2

While none is needed, we will soon see clear proof of God's allowing evil to continue on in the World even after the Flood. Indeed, God is permitting Satan to continue to be Prince of the Air - subject to certain restraints - but only "for a time" which will be through all of Act I. We should also note that God has reserved Satan's epic act of evil for Scene 3, but more on that later.

Scene 2 of Act I begin with the survival of Noah and his 3 sons, the forerunners of the World's three (3) major groupings of people: Gentile (Japheth), Hamitic (Ham) and Semitic (Shem). Off and on these three groups are in conflict, with most of the hostility being between the Semites (focused on modern day Israel), and the Hamites (focused on the modern-day forces of radical Islam). The intense hostility between these two was originally triggered by Abraham's disobedience of God, and God's prophecy that enmity exists and continues throughout Act I. Despite his sins Abraham grew to develop a very faithful relationship with God, and God chose Abraham and the Semitic people out of which would come the nation Israel and through whose people God would reveal Himself, the Messiah as Savior of the World, and God's Plan for all of mankind. The zenith of Abraham's faithfulness occurred when Abraham was prepared to sacrifice to God the life of his beloved son Isaac until God prevented or enabled Abraham from doing so. Of course, Abraham's intended act foreshadowing of the incredible love of God when He went on to allow the sacrificial death of His only son, Jesus - in Scene 3, Act I - to enable the only means possible for reconciling sinful man and Holy God.

---

5.   See I Peter 3:10

D. Observations of Act I, Scene 3

Scene 3 brings the long-awaited and prophesied Messiah, narrating his birth, life, teachings, crucifixion and finally defeating death by His Resurrection. As with Joseph's betrayal by his brothers, if there was ever something intended for bad that was turned into good, it was Satan's orchestration of the crucifixion - an act intended to defeat God's Messiah. Of course, this epic act of evil of Satan's career served only as the precursor event to what would become the single most important and central event in all of World History, namely crucifixion followed by the bodily Resurrection of Jesus![6] One can only imagine the surprise and shock of Satan believing he had "out-maneuvered" his rival, God. The Resurrection event is well described as "central" - for it occurs roughly in the middle of human history and at a time of relative peace (the peace of Rome) when such an event could take with notice, and at a geographical place that was situated in the center of civilization surrounded by connecting roadway systems further aiding rapid communication of this pivotal event in all history.[7]

Critically, with Jesus' Resurrection and then Ascension, God ushered the Holy Spirit's coming into all of the World to accomplish His purposes. As Jesus said:

> "It is for your good that I am going away, unless I go away, the Counselor [Advocate, Holy Comforter, Helper] will not come to you." (Jo 16:7)[8]

Shortly following the Resurrection of Jesus, God inspired the New Testament narratives to be written beginning with many of Jesus' Apostles and several of His former enemies or non-believers all testifying to Jesus as Messiah by virtue of both their writings and the giving up of their lives. Particularly noteworthy is Paul's testimony - a dedicated teacher of the Jewish law and sworn enemy of Jesus, who after witnessing Jesus' appearance, went on to both dedicate and sacrifice his very life for Jesus and the Gospel message. Additionally, the conversion of James, Jesus' brother, who prior to Jesus' resurrection was never a Believer (What, my brother!) but following not only believed, but eventually also gave his life for the Gospel message (along with all of Jesus' Apostles excepting John who was banished to the Isle of Patmos).

While God allows a restrained Satan to continue on after Jesus' Ascension, the Holy Spirit's introduction into the world will safeguard all wearing the cloak of Jesus and possessing the power of the indwelling Holy Spirit.

---

6. Next to the creation, the Resurrection of Jesus Christ is the single most important event in History. See the Author's Book, "Resurrection - Fact or Fiction? A Trial Lawyer Looks at all the Evidence", Westbow Press, 2015.

7. Jerusalem was close to the Center of the civilized World and during a time of relative peace with vast road way-communications thanks to Rome's, Caesar and Alexander the Great, and also the Greek language.

8. Unlike Jesus in the flesh, the Holy Spirit can appear and be available to one, many, and all at the very same time. He is also the Commander in Chief of all spiritual warfare, and as such unequaled by anything Satan can bring to bear.

E. Observations of Act I, Scene 4

One of the principal themes throughout History- a theme that continues today and will continue throughout Act I - is the hostility among the 3 peoples, Gentiles, Hamites and Semites, and, primarily between the two latter peoples. This enmity was triggered when Abraham became impa¬tient with God's promise of a child and disobeyed God. Asa result of his sin Ishmael was born to Abraham and his servant Hagar and a few years later, God fulfilled His promise with the birth of Isaac to Abraham and his wife Sarah. Ishmael's faith ultimately came under the umbrella of Allah and Muhammad who formalized the Islamic faith under the Quran. Since roughly 650 A.D. the militant Jihadic element of Islam has essentially declared war against the "Jew and the Infidel," seeking to "Islamatize" the entire World. Nonetheless, the majority of Muslims today are peace-loving, wishing to have no part in militant Jihadism, and many are converting to the Christian faith,

One need only observe the Mid-East - among other spots in the World today - to see this des¬ tined hostility between the issue of Ishmael and Isaac continuing to play out. Currently, the radical elements of Islam, epitomized by Iran's leadership, vow to destroy Israel. Israel returned to Nationhood in 1948 after nearly 2,000 years of dispersion following 70 AD. Scripture suggests that never again will there not be a Jewish Nation. As we know, a key campaign objective for these two antagonists has been to secure all of Jerusalem as situs for their Temple, and geo¬ graphical center point of their faith.

Of course, after the completion of Messiah's earthly mission in 30 AD, followed by the horrific destruction of the Temple and Jerusalem in 70 AD along with as many as a million Jews the ongoing hostility between radical Islam and Israel, while very real to each is largely symbolic to the Church. In God's church, Jesus is now the temple and the center of worship, so any meaning of having a temple or even a temple in Jerusalem is symbolic and has been voided with Messiah's appearance with Jesus making it clear that our bodies are the true temples of God. Further, there is "neither" Jew nor Gentile, slave nor free male nor female, since with God and the Church, made up of regenerated hearts there can be no prejudice.[9] Nevertheless, the defeat of those seeking to overcome Israel and take control of Jerusalem remains a significant symbolic event which will be highlighted with Jesus' second coming and a final battle, whether of Armageddon or other, representing the salvation and victory of God's church.[10]

As such, relative to God's Plan the major and most substantive narrative in Scene 4 is the ongoing work of the Great Commission and the spread of the Gospel and Christian Church world-wide. Despite this narrative being the underlying theme of God's purpose, it receives little attention nor even recognition by the World's media forces. Instead, the media spotlight shines on the side-shows of violence, focusing instead on the various evil themes in the World.[11]

---

9.   Gal. 3:28

10.   See "The Apocalypse Code," by Hank Hanegraaff, Thomas Nelson, 2007.

11.   Today's "Free Reporting" Press is neither "Free" in the sense of being independent of agenda and or being the true voice of the people, nor objective reporting in the sense of any comprehensive, in depth, reporting of the true facts. In this regard, we hear bias not objectivity, and mostly bad, not good acts nor actors. If we actually heard (or saw) all of the really good actors and good acts that occur every minute of each day in this World, many would view people, God and all of life very differently. Accordingly, major media entities must be seen as private, profit-making enterprises each having its own agenda and cause.

Accordingly, the truly big media story and "breaking news" should be the fact that even in the presence of evil and with Satan "in control" of the World, the Messianic message and all of its derivative influences for good in the World have not only continued to spread World-wide throughout Act I it far outweighs all evil.

Further, while arguably on a lesser scale than previously, the continuing of this "God-dominance" and prevalence of good, charity and love in this World needs to be recognized by all actors as illustrative of God's power and plan. With Messiah's "defeat" of Satan and preventing Satan from ever being able to overcome the Church, there has been no need for God's time to formally reign as King of the World, instead, allowing God to continue His plan to evidence His power through the prevalence of Messiah's disciples and the indwelling Holy Spirit in the World. What incredible real Life/Play witness to the love, power, control and plan of Almighty God.[12]

At this point, let's pause and dwell further on the fact that you/we are all present actors on stage during this Scene 4, and we should recognize this perspective and the opportunity that this live Play in progress provides for each of us "to act" on His behalf! We must also take note that Scene 4 will soon end and that Scene S with its violence culmination fast approaching.

A word about wealth, possessions, money - or anything that possesses us, other than Christ. Don't let this become "our score card," as one of America's richest men recently said.

Instead dwell on Jesus' reply to the rich young man who asked: "What must I do to get eternal life."

Jesus replied:

"If you want to be perfect, go sell your possessions and give to the poor, and you will have treasure in Heaven."

---

12. As any military commander knows, to defeat an enemy one needs to first identify and know the enemy. Most of the world's nations and peoples visualize their enemies as "flesh and blood." However, they are not; rather, the world's meaningful battles are all spiritual in nature, which is why when Jesus ascended, God unleashed the Triune's spiritual force - the Holy Spirit - into the world. A Comforter, Counselor and Protector who can be in one or all places at one time. Satan, neither omnipresent nor omnipotent is no match, and while already defeated, he is not yet vanquished, and so he fights on, securing casualties on the world's battlefields, one at a time. However, Satan's arrows are unable to pierce those wearing the Armor of God, nor can he ever pre¬ vail against God's church. No surprise since Holy omnipotent God is also the creator/father of all military stratagems.
Also, see Footnote II

"I tell you the truth, it is hard for a rich man to enter the Kingdom of Heaven. ..it is easier for a camel to go through the eye of a needle than for a rich man to enter the Kingdom of God."[13]

Warnings against Being "of the World"

God's Word is clear - Christ's followers are commanded to not become engaged in the world or its politics. Christians are citizens of God's Kingdom, who are only passing through the world, a world where Satan has been permitted - for a time - to govern as the evil prince of the air. God's Children are given strict warnings, including:

Is 13:7: _"I will punish the world for its evil."_
Is 13: u: _"My Kingdom is not of this world."_

John 15:18-19: _"If the world hates you, keep in mind that it hated me first...you_ do not belong to the world, but I have chosen you out of the world..." James 4:4: _'½nyone who chooses to be a friend_ of the world becomes an enemy of God."

I John 2:15:   _"Do not love the world, or anything in it. If anyone loves the_ world, the love of the Father is not in him."

John 3:16:   _"For God so loved the (people in the) world that He gave His only son_ that whoever believes in Him shall not perish but have eternal life".

One evening of watching cable news will convince anyone of the wisdom of God's command to be not "of" this world. It will also remind us of Messiah's prophecy that though open to all, "only a few will enter the small gate on the narrow road. "Matt. 1:14

A reasonable estimate of authentic Christians within the world today would be 10% and decreasing. This fact alone explains much of what is seen in the world today.

The Mission of Christians

So, what does Jesus and scripture teach Christians to do while passing through the world on their way to Eternal Life in God's Kingdom? Christians are commissioned to spread the Gospel of Peace, to represent "The Way," to be and to teach "salt and light," to feed and care for the poor and needy, and to always serve as examples of Christian ship. Christians must never give politics the opportunity to distort or malign Christ and His mission.

As such, there is the more invisible but permanent Kingdom of God and light - co-existing for the present time - with the very visible but temporal World of darkness, evil and Satan.

The children of God and the citizens of the world pursue totally different basic missions, as well as destinies - either Eternal Life or Eternal Death each being the result of each individual's free¬ will choice.

---

13.   Matt. 19:16-2

Christian Engagement in the World

So, what are Christians in America permitted and required to do relative to the world and our nation?

> _"Render to Caesar the things that are Caesar's and to God the things that are God's"_
> _Matt 22:21 "Let every person be in subjection to the governing authorities." Romans 13:1._

Christians passing through the U.S. owe to its governmental bodies obedience to the laws, including payment of taxes, and compliance with any required military service. All else is owed to God, including dedication to work, fulfillment of one's life plan, providing for one's family and the poor, spreading the Gospel, and living a Christian life.

Voting?

What about "voting" for various political offices-including the President? Voting is not required as a matter of obedience to either God or the nation's laws, voting being a privilege, not a man¬ date of any authority. What is clear is that if one chooses to vote it should be done privately as an individual, and never "on behalf of Christianity;" the "Christian right," nor on the basis of trying to vote for the "best Christian" or even "a Christian."

All persons - Christian or not - sin, and sin is sin. Further, in voting for President one is not voting for a Chief Priest, or even the more Christian-like as between two individuals. Rather, the President's role as Chief Executive Officer and Commander -in-Chief of the Armed Forces embodies at most 2 or 3 basic missions. Accordingly, one's choice should ideally be the person most capable, and thoroughly committed to:

A) securing and keeping the peace, just as the Pax Romana and prior to that the conquests of Alexander the Great brought peace - knowing that Peace is paramount both to achieve its inherent benefits, as well as to enable the spread of the Gospel of Peace; and

B) enabling free enterprise to function and thrive without governmental interference, and with government providing only those services for which it is best suited, including maintaining the armed forces, post offices, public schools, utilities, highways, etc.

One thing absolutely certain is the fact that elected central government was never intended to be the creator or guardian of the people's mores or cultural/societal standards of conduct nor was government ever intended to provide goods, benefits, or services - including health care, social security etc. Cultural/societal standards and mores can only flow from God - through scripture and the "salt and light" spread by Jesus and His Christian disciples.

But is Not America - A Christian Nation?

It is worth noting that America's central government was neither founded nor structured as a "Christian Nation." Indeed, many of our U.S. Constitutional provisions would violate Christian teachings, including its initial allowing of slaves - all despite our Declaration of Independence citing that "all men are created equal."

Additionally, there are the First Amendment rights of "Freedom" of Religion(s), Speech, and Petition along with the Second Amendment right of the people to bear arms. Also, there was that "little matter" of secession and the Civil War fought over slavery, resulting in killing more Americans than all of the wars in history.

Be further assured that our nation and its politics did not just recently become so demonstrably worldly and sinful. Ben Franklin (a great uncle) was a wise forefather, but he was also a deist, an adulterer and cut his beloved (and illegitimate) son, William, out of his estate long after the war ended because William had been a crown loyalist. The presidential campaign against John Adams' second term, waged by Thomas Jefferson -

another deist, adulterer, slaveholder, etc. is widely regarded as one of the most vicious in American history. Abe Lincoln was viciously attacked by his opponents as less than man and was portrayed as an ape in a New York news¬ paper. While as great as he was and against slavery, Lincoln felt that African Americans were inferior and should not vote.

Accordingly, all of the years have only confirmed the world's evil, and never more evident than in its politics. Indeed, the world's "poster child" for political evil is when the world's only perfect man, moral teacher, doer of miracles and, indeed, God in the flesh appeared 2,000 years ago, and despite seeking no political power, was falsely accused, beaten and crucified!

Salt, Light and Salvation Is Messiah Christ's Plan

As noted above, Christians are not to sleep-walk as they pass through the world; rather they are to represent and disciple "salt and light." As "Salt," the spread and preservation of the Christian faith and the Gospel, both in the world and forever. As "Light" of the world, Jesus once ascended, made His disciples the sons of Light and enlightenment for the world. As such, Christians are to "be fruitful and multiply" - work and raise families in traditional family units and churches - God's key entities for social stability, raising and educating the young with God's wisdom, and perpetuating the Christian light.

The Twin Supports

Early America knew well the truth of God's Word, including - "The fear of the Lord is the beginning of Wisdom" (Ps. III:IO). George Washington correctly stated that religion and morality are the indispensable supports for American government, noting that morality cannot be maintained without the Christian religion. Note well that these two supports come not from within government, but rather from Christians outside of both government and politics. As these foundational supports weaken or fail, so will the stability and viability of America's government.

Take note that most political activists tend to be younger, "uneducated," self-centered and self-promotional - functioning largely as unwise dwarfs when it comes to our Creator God, "His Story," Scripture, Judea - Christianity morality, early America and its founding and/or history of the world. Additionally lacking is the increasing loss of the critical role of the traditional family unit together with all of the essential educational fundamentals of wisdom not being t aught in most universities- all necessary for the faithful and responsible exercise of America's individ¬ual freedoms and responsibilities.

Also, unknown is Gal. 3:28 which confirms that among Christians- "_There is neither Jew nor Greek, slave nor free, male or female - for we are all one in Christ Jesus._" While this settles all of the issues regarding the existence of any individual differences once and for all, the <u>only</u> way for this principle to become ingrained is through its invasion into the human heart along with the Holy Spirit - certainly never by means of superficial mandates suggested by self-serving, progressive politicians espousing individual warfare, partisanship and socialism.

F. Observations of Act I, Scene 5

Many - if not most agree - that our current Scene 4 will include near its end the "latter days." Scene 5 will present the "last days" - relatively brief and filled with trials and tribulations, preceding Jesus' second corning in Act II .

Scene 5's "last days" will likely be largely, but not solely, geographically and symbolically cen¬tered on the Nation of Israel and the broader Mid-East. However, be assured that these days bring difficult times world-wide, including America.

Theologians provide us with essentially three (3) views of these last days, based on variances in interpretations of Biblical prophecy, principally centered on defining the nature, time and location of the Tribulation and the battle(s) commonly referred to as Armageddon.

Perhaps the oldest and most classic view is that Armageddon has already occurred, and refers to what was perhaps the most devastating event in the World at the time - namely the Romans ' destruction of the second Temple and much of Jerusalem in 70 AD. This view centers on Jesus' comments possibly in (ca.) 27 AD[14] which are believed to refer to the near future 70 AD even ts, combined with the belief that John wrote his "Revelations" before 70 AD (most likely between 55 and 65 AD), since nowhere in Revelation is there any reference to these major events occurring in 70AD.

More recent views see Armageddon as intending to reference still future events to occur in the "last days," likely in Scene 5. This view holds to times of Tribulation anticipated to last for a total period of 7 years, with the last 3 ½ years being the times of Great Tribulation perhaps triggered in large part by the "Rapture" - a moment when all Christians are "taken up," suddenly van¬ishing from the World stage leaving evil rampant. Further, the geographical (in part symbolic) center-point of these Armageddon events will be Israel and the Mid-East, where after a time of relative peace for Israel, war erupts. In the last or 7th year, Israel's enemies combine, seeking to destroy Israel - the Nation Israel or all people of God - but are stopped by direct action of the Messiah, returning now as powerful conqueror, not a babe in the manger. Messiah calls down fire from above to defeat the attacking armies, culminating in the death of perhaps one-third of all peoples including the huge forces seeking to destroy "Israel" whether for reasons of religious dominance, seeking land, oil, warm seaports, or out of mere hostility led by Satan.

The third, and somewhat middle view is perhaps the most likely with some adaptation. Based on both Old Testament and New Testament Scripture interpretations together with viewing world history, events over the past 75years, along with current Mid-East and world-wide developments, Scene 5 will seem most likely to portray the following features and events unfolding on stage:

1. fulfillment of the "Christian Church" age with ever increasing converts, most of which are likely to come from beyond America's borders, including in particular, Africa, China, and even the Mid-East; (See Matt. 34:14)

2. increasingly violent acts of God's environmental forces of nature, including earth¬ quakes, famines, etc. (See Matt. 24; Jer.14:16; Rev. 8, 11:13)

3. increasing man-led violence world-wide, with many major events centered around the Nation Israel, the Mid-East and environs;

4. an indefinite, but relatively brief time of Trials and Tribulation, including a point in time when all genuine followers of Christ on stage may be gathered up and vanish from the World stage (raptured), leaving all those remaining on stage in the midst of evil which can now run ram pant,[15] and

5. a culminating, combined-nation military confrontation with the Nation Israel; (Iran's current leadership promises to destroy Israel along with the U.S. as "Satan"); any such attack is promised to be defeated -with "Israel" God's people being saved - all incidental to Messiah's return and direct intervention, utilizing fire ("never again destruction by flood") called from above.

---

14.   See Matt. 24:33 re: "this generation..."

15.   Re: Rapture: occurring Pre-or Mid-Tribulation, however, the only Rapture may well occur only at the end when those who have died in Christ are raised, followed by the Rapture. At the second coming of the Lord, all brothers in Christ "who are still alive, who are left, will be caught up in the air... while (other) people are saying 'peace and safety' destruction will come on them suddenly: • I Thess: 4-5

Scene 5 will be the shortest Scene in the Play whether lasting 7 years or less. This is fortunate, given that Scene 5 is almost certain to be the most difficult and violent in God's Play.

Note also that while many of the actors still on stage in Scene 5 will likely vanish or be raptured from the stage not to be seen again Until Act III, many may also re-appear near the very end of Scene 5, appearing now in indestructible bodily form as part of Messiah's Army- all in fulfillment of God's promise to preserve His People.[16]

G. Observations of Act II

Act II begins with the second coming or return of Messiah -who will rule from Jerusalem - and who along with His Disciples will ultimately administer the Great Judgment of all actors - all people who have appeared on stage in God's Play over its some 5,000 plus years.

Note: Regarding "The Millennium"

There are perhaps 3 or 4 versions put forth by Theologians of what has been commonly referenced as the Millennium - reference to the "1,000 year" period cited in Revelations 20. Some project the time period as a precise 1,000 years, while others believe it represents an indefinite period of time.

The oldest view adopts an indefinite period. It cites Jesus' reference in Matt. 24:34 to "this generation" as referring to the generation there existent (in 70 AD} and that the future Armageddon type events being described by Jesus refer to the Romans' destruction of the Temple and much of Jerusalem that would and did occur in 70 AD. Pursuant to this view Jesus ' Return and Second Coming can be virtually any time now followed by Jesus' reign, the Judgment and then Heaven/Act III.

This view further incorporates all of the time between Jesus' two appearances into the period of time in which we now live and are on stage. While it is a time during which Satan is the ruling Prince of the Air, Satan is also being restricted and bound by God from allowing him to thwart God's Plan or growth of His church world-wide.[17]

A second, and a bit more recent view is that the period between Jesus's two (2) appearances is the "Church" age, including this time in Scene 4 in which we are currently on stage. While this view is much the same as the first above, it is believed that there is yet to come a "great revival," following which Jesus will then return to administer the final Judgment preceding Heaven or Act III.

> Note: Of course, any such revival could well be centered less in America and more world-wide, e.g., Africa, China, and Mid-East where millions are being converted to Christianity annually.

The third and more recent view is that while Jesus will return almost any time now, His return will be followed by a total binding of Satan until near the very end of 1,000 years with Jesus' ruling the World from "Jerusalem" for a precise period of 1,000 years, follow¬ing which will come the final Judgment and then Heaven, Act Ill.

In connection with both of these latter views, many believe that the final, "last days" and Armageddon events will, as described above, be centered on the Nation Israel and the surrounding Mid-East which, will occur just preceding Jesus' second coming.

---

16. See Genesis, Isaiah, Ezekiel, Daniel, Revelations, et al.

17. "on this rock (Jesus, Son of God) I will build my church, and the gates of Hades (powers of death or forces opposed to Christ) will not overcome it." (Matt. r6:18-19) While the Catholic Church interprets the rock here as "petros" or Peter (as opposed to "Petra") this in no way detracts from any authority of the Catholic Church. All faithful Christian churches derive free expression of faith in Jesus as the Messiah, Son of the Living God and the foundation laid by Christ and His apostles, plus the prophets.

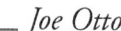

Note: While some - if not much of this seems a bit vague or indefinite it is perhaps intentionally so but be assured that the ultimate events of Jesus' second coming, the Final Judgment and Heaven are "written in stone" - or "the blood of Jesus!"

H. Observations of Act III

The Final Act, III, is Heaven, will take place right here on the stage of Earth, or as Scripture states- a "new Earth" and not necessarily out in space somewhere! However, it will be a renewed Earth, a Garden o, f Eden, returned to its original state. (A real "greening "by the original creator of all green!) Some believe that Heaven will be "a new Jerusalem, lowered from above, a cube like affair measuring 1,500 miles in each dimension!" Regardless, it will surely be, as they say, "Heaven on Earth!"

Satan will be forever destroyed having been thrown into the eternal "Lake of Burning Sulfur:' With all things now perfect and God/Messiah/Holy Spirit - the Triune God - serving in perfect Kingship, this final Act III will endure FOREVER AND EVER!! It will also be the most exciting, creative, active, satisfying - and worshipful - time one can imagine - and no one can![18]

As He has made clear, God truly wishes all actors to re-appear in Act III. Unfortunately, most will not. Oddly enough, most actors neither seek nor elect Christ as savior. Reason given include "I'm busy; like my life; Lies; maybe later" as such, know that God will always honor the free will choice of his created souls. All of this is vitally critical to note, since Act III is the final Act, the final opportunity to be on stage and to elect to live a "Heavenly" life that will be eternal.

---

18.   The process is actually one of election by God, prior to each of us being born. While correct theological explanation, this election process is perhaps best understood as a form of God's foreknowledge, knowing in advance each actor and each actor's role performance to come on the World stage.

Let's look further at why those actors who will not re-appear in Act III will not do so.

First: Many actors choose to follow what they believe to be a different way to Heaven - sometimes through a different faith, religion or philosophy- rather than following "The Way," and the "only way" offered by God the son, Jesus Christ; (Satan's biggest lie is that all religions will get you to Heaven);

Second: Many actors feel they are "good" people entitled to Heaven: 'I'm as good as any other actor; surely I will be invited to appear in Heaven's Act III." Surprisingly, some of these folks even express that they have never "sinned against God".

Third: Incredibly, many actors reject "Heaven" as a place they even wish to go. "What and sit on a cloud all day!" Or they might say, "I want to focus on this life, in the here and now, to the fullest"; and/or

Fourth: Some actors will claim "ignorance of the law," that they have never been taught and/ or have never had the time to learn or understand God's Plan; they have missed the fact that God's Plan (and His Play) while open to all, nevertheless prescribes an exclusive, distinct, and only "way" to re-appear in Act III/Heaven.

Once again, we emphasize the fact that the current "window of opportunity to Live Forever" and re-appear on stage in Act III - which Act will then endure throughout Eternity - is a window that was first opened several thousand years ago. Further, while it remains open yet today, this window will close suddenly and forever.

For those currently on stage, including you and me, the window will close at the moment we draw our last breath.

IV. GOD'S PLAY LASTS THOUSANDS OF YEARS - WHY SO LONG?

First, because God knew each one of us before being born and wanted each of us to be on stage to playout and contribute our individual life's roles and have an opportunity for Eternal Life. God is a God of creativity and knew in advance what each of His children would bring to the stage. He wanted the World to see and experience what each of the actors could/would create, cause or effect to advance His Kingdom - a cause and effect that could/would be repeated time and again, all for His purposes and Kingdom.

Of the millions, three (3) quick vivid examples will illustrate man's creative inventions, causes and effects. First, Guttenberg's printing press - not invented until 1450 - but once it was, Bibles could be printed en masse. As a result, the Bible has easily become the World's biggest bookseller each year. Imagine, the number of people that the Guttenberg Press has helped to assure being on stage for Act III!

Second, the Internet, and its offspring. While the number of actor's who will have been helped through technology and/or social media to re-appear on stage in Act III might be than the Guttenberg Press, it may nevertheless be substantial.

Third, while Heaven will have no need for medical advancements in Act III - many folks will particularly owe their presence in Act III to the many miracles of medicine and/or caregivers experienced in Act I.

Finally, are you not over-joyed that God's Play is still going on for your sake or the sake of sal¬vation of your children, grandchildren? How sad - nay, tragic - it will be when all comes to an end, and no further actors will be able to appear on the World's stage and/or try out for re-ap¬pearance in ACT III.

V. GOD IS A LOVING GOD!

The answer to whether God is a loving God is certain - He is! Exhibit A is God "allowing" His sinless (and only) son to be beaten and crucified to death (imagine, your allowing - indeed your choosing - your son to be killed so a neighbor's child might live!) Further, God planned and prophesied it all in order to provide a way, and the only way possible - for a God who is Holy and Just - to enable sinful man, you and me - to escape the ultimate just punishment[19] of eternal death. This "way" is for sinful man - unable to do anything to justify himself - to put on the cloak of the sinless Messiah - Jesus Christ - thereby taking on His righteousness and to become worthy, justified, righteous, cleansed, atoned, and forgiven. As a result, man is thereby through the Grace of God - gifted with Heaven - an invitation to go on stage for all of Act III - for all of Eternity!

However, please note that while man's means and way to Heaven is offered to us as a gift of grace from a loving God -while free to us, very costly to God - but as with any gift man needs to evidence his sincere intent and act of acceptance of this gift - in both head and heart - a heart that becomes regenerated, through the indwelling Holy Spirit which in turn conforms one's mind. This heart regeneration will not only demand and command man to act - it delights man through an acting out of his new faith by acts of love for God and fellow man.

Exhibit Bis God's loving wish to have everyone who was ever born, and who has ever appeared on stage in His Play to re-appear on stage for Act III, i.e., to have life eternal in Heaven. God clearly states that He "wishes none to perish and for all to enter the Kingdom of God."[20] Note further that God's plan of salvation is open to all, regardless of race, nationality or status.

Exhibit C is God's extreme patience! God has been patient to allow as many people as possible, to have opportunity over their entire lifetime to seek Him and to accept God's offer and His wish for our Eternal life. Clear evidence of this is that you and I are now here on stage perhaps 5,000 years after the Garden of Eden - still being provided with the opportunity to appear in Act III. Of course, at some point this window of opportunity will close, but in the meantime, it will not end until we take our last breath or the end of Act II, since salvation is effective and effectually the same whether one receives it at age IO or 100.

VI. GOD HATES EVIL

It is equally clear that God hates evil. Exhibit A was God banning the rebellious Lucifer from Heaven. Exhibit B was God banning man - after he sinned - from the Garden of Eden. While God has promised to put an end to Satan forever this will not occur until God's purposes and plans are fulfilled. Exhibit C is God's promise to bring a permanent end to Satan (and all of his demon followers) just prior to Act III. In this connection, Heaven (Act III) by its nature, purpose and eternal duration will (finally) neither admit nor permit evil, death, nor sickness - indeed, not even tears!

Many people cite as their reason(s) for not believing in a God, the fact that there is so much evil in the World and /or that any good God would not allow any evil. However, stop and think - or as God has said, "Be still and know that I am God." We argue the above only because of our rebel¬ lion, our not knowing the Word of

---

19.   Understand that one can also be punished by or in the World for his/her sin, whether by law, others, oneself, one's conscience, circumstances of life, or one's failure to seek the forgiveness and salvation of God.

20.   "[The Lord]...is patient with you, not wanting anyone to perish, but wanting everyone to come to repentance."
(2 Pet. 3:9).

God, our foolishness and/or our impatience as a result of which we do not know, have not seen, appreciated, or understood God's full Plan, and His Life's Play as being presented here.

In response you may say, O.K. - I understand God's banning of all evil later, but why has God allowed evil, and indeed much evil, throughout all of Act I! A full appreciation and understand¬ ing of God's Play will clearly persuade us that even Act I demonstrate both a loving God and a God who hates evil.

In partial response, perhaps the single most surprising and insightful observation of Act I of God's Play is that God has not allowed - and currently is not allowing in Scene 4 - total free reign to Satan and Evil - as an observer might initially conclude or argue. Absolute proof of this fact could come in Scene S when the "Rapture" occurs. At the Rapture, it is believed by many, that all of God's children - all who have undergone the conversion experience of a regenerated heart and a transformed mind, having come to accept and follow Messiah-Christ as Savior and Lord
-and who are then on stage in Scene 5 - will suddenly vanish, leaving only those actors who are not - or not yet - children of God.

Then, and only then, for the very first time in World history, not only will evil be present but only evil will be present, and evil enabled to run rampant with a different result no one will mistake! This is not to say that there will not be "good." Indeed, many will be likely to find and turn to God during this time, perhaps recognizing the error of their ways more clearly than ever before, and for the first time.

Accordingly, we need to observe and understand that while God has indeed allowed Satan to have "control" of the World, and has mostly restrain ed Himself from asserting His own direct acts and controls in Act I,[21] not for a moment has God given Satan and evil free reign in Act I. (Recall how God restrained Satan from taking Job's life, but allowed Satan to take from Job virtually all that Job possessed - his children, his land, good health, etc.)

Indeed, it will come as a surprise to many that Act I of God's Play and Plan has had in part a purpose of demonstrating the overcoming effect and influence of God's power despite Satan's "rule" and without God taking direct control as a King. Thus, the forces loosed in the world following Jesus Christ's 3-year ministry, namely the arrival and presence of the Holy Spirit/Counselor, Advocate and Comforter which in conjunction with all of the inspired work of Messiah's disciples and the converted hearts of millions of God's children have all contributed to God's con¬ trolling and limiting evil.

---

21.   Actually there have been many times and moments even in Act 1 when God has exercised His omnipotent power directly, though not always in obvious fashion. The most obvious examples are often through con¬ trolling the forces of nature or directing what can only be termed a miracle. Of course, there are the many miracles performed by Jesus during His 3-year ministry in Scene 3. Note that all of the forces of nature are direct acts of God designed to accomplish His purpose. Perhaps less obvious are all of those day-to-day incredible little acts that only God could have caused or arranged, often in direct response to Prayer. Many of us have experienced these events and moments, but too rarely do we credit them to God as "God experiences" - rather we ascribe them to "good luck", or "coincidences."(There is no word for coincidence in ancient Hebrew.) Watch for these, as they happen and when they do always give thanks to our loving God.

Recall just 3 of the mor e dramatic "Acts of God:"
        the Flood destroying evil peoples in Scene 1
        the Red Sea's sudden rising waters drowning out Pharaoh's Army chasing, Israelites in Scene 2;
        Crumbling (earthquake?) of the Walls of Jericho.

Accordingly, while refraining from taking direct, first-hand or overt rule, God has demonstrated that even His indirect power, presence and purposes far exceed anything that Satan and his demonic followers could ever do. Recall well Messiah's words:

> "On this rock (Jesus Christ - not Peter) I will build my church and the gates of Hades will not overcome it."[22]

> "It is for your good that I am going away. Unless I go away, the Counselor (Advocate, Holy Comforter, Helper, Spirit) will not come to you. When he comes, he will convict the world of guilt in regard to sin, righteousness and judgment - because the prince of this world now stands condemned... 'and...' when the Spirit of t ruth comes he will guide you into all truth."[23]

VII. Why Does God Allow Any Evil[24] In Act I - Even If The Good Outweighs All The Bad? Why Did GOD CREATE LUCIFER IN THE FIRST PLACE?

It is understood that all of this may still leave many with the "$64,000 Question," saying -

"OK, I now understand that God's Plan and Play is to keep evil out of most of Act II and that evil will be totally absent in Act III; further, I can now also accept the fact that God

- both directly and indirectly - has caused good to overcome and limit much evil in Act

I but, pray tell why does God allow any evil in Act I? Could not God accomplish His purposes without allowing any evil?"

The short answer to the question - "Could God accomplish His purpose and Plan without ever allowing evil into the World?" - is NO! Certainly not for a Holy and Just God, nor a God who has created man with an independent, very strong and Free Will be capable of rejecting God and His commands.

Yes, God could have created things - including man - in such a way as to virtually compel man to follow God. Thus, God could have created either or both an environment without evil, or man without free will. But, to what end? A mere exercise in foregone conclusions, or robot-like obedience of man to God? Further, much of what is described below relative to the purposes of evil, and the good that comes from evil throughout Act I would be lost. Finally, man's choice and election to follow God would be rendered hollow and meaningless.

Recall that in the beginning, God created man with his free and independent will in the Garden of Eden, and also exposed man to evil in the form of Satan as a serpent. Man chose to listen and follow the serpent's lie about God. In consequence, God ejected man from the Garden and has allowed man to be exposed to the evil that man chose to remain in the World.[25]

Of course, all of this further begs the question of why God created the beautiful Lucifer in the first place when God knew that Lucifer would want to become like God, be ejected from Heaven, become Satan, the "father of all lies," and ultimately lead much of mankind away from the narrow path and onto the wide pathway leading to death.

22.   Matt. 16: 18-19. Also see FN 16
23.   Jo 16:7-13
24.   or similarly, pain in our lives.
25.   And along with ejectment from the Garden of Eden, God mandated death to men, and
        to men: "painful toil," and "sweat of your brow".
        to women: "I will greatly increase your pains in childbearing" et al. (Gen. 3:16-19)

Given man's human nature, including his free and independent Will, God did and does choose to use evil (along with man's human infirmities and nature) to do its work in order to accomplish God's purposes. Often these purposes are not always understood, particularly over the short term, and maybe not even until we receive enlightenment in Act III. However, this Play presentation should help to provide significant insight into God's purposes for evil, how God uses evil, and why God has permitted evil to exist in the World - though only throughout Act I and for a brief time in Act II.

Beyond the above, first and foremost, fundamental, sine qua non justification and the post¬ merchild for the purpose of evil in Act I is found in Scene 3, when Satan's acts produced the events

leading to Jesus Christ 's crucifixion and death - with Satan thinking he had finally out-witted and defeated God's plan and indeed, God Himself.

Imagine Satan's face when he learned of Jesus' Resurrection! If ever you wanted proof that Satan was/is not privy to the future and God's plan of salvation this is surely it.

Thus, if God had had no other reason for creating Lucifer/Satan, Jesus' sacrificial and redemp¬tive death followed by His bodily resurrection - the center point of all human history - these events providing for man's atonement with God were justification enough.

Beyond even the case of Joseph and his jealous brothers, was there ever such an event in human history so purely undeserved, so unjust and evil, and an event Satan meant for evil but that God, the master chess player, used for good! Not only good, but the essential "life-saving" good of all time!

Note further that even Jesus in the midst of this turning point in all History which he fully knew, nevertheless while enduring His human agony and suffering uttered the following:

"Father, let this cup pass from me." and
"Father, why have you forsaken me?"

Is it any wonder that these same words often pass through our lips as we "toil," "sweat," suffer pain or evil? Also, like Satan, most often it is difficult for us to see the good that God causes to arise from evil - even to those who love God and obey Him. Nevertheless, good is caused, and the very first thing on which we focus when confronted by pain or evil is the cross and God's faithful promises.

Of course, these events of evil producing good are many and constant, even if not always as dramatic or meaningful as Jesus and Joseph. Nevertheless, God allows pain in our lives to produce good and/or to show God's power. Three (3) examples will further illustrate the point, the first two coming from Scripture, and the third testimony from more recent times.

<u>First, from the Old Testament - Job:</u>

Job was a man greatly blessed by God with a large family, land and possessions. Satan challenged God saying that Job loves God only because God greatly Blessed Him, and if Job were to lose all that he possessed, Job would curse God. God responded to Satan by allowing Satan to cause Job to suffer as Satan wished, limited only by preventing Satan from taking Job's life - another example of God's limitations imposed on Satan. Thereafter, Job was caused to lose his entire family, all of his possessions and suffer from bodily sores, despite all of which Job continued to love and serve God.

Not unlike Jesus, in the midst of his crisis Job stated:

"Though He slay me, yet will I trust in Him." [Job 13:15]

<u>Second, from the New Testament, Paul:</u>

Paul, formerly Saul, was Jesus' principal enemy - until being converted by the resurrected Jesus, to becoming the Gospel's strongest, and most effective disciple at the most critical time in the history of Christianity. Paul had a serious physical infirmity (unidentified in scripture), described only as a "thorn in his flesh." Despite Paul being totally faithful to serving God and spreading the Gospel of Christ and praying three (3) times (perhaps many more) for God to remove his "thorn" God did not. Nevertheless, Paul carried on throughout perhaps even more strongly because of his infirmity.

Paul, in his suffering, reports God saying to him -

"My grace is sufficient for you - for my power is made perfect in (your) weakness." [2 Cor. 12:9]

Paul further relates:

"That is why- for Christ's sake - I delight in weaknesses, in insults, in hardships, in persecutions, in difficulties. For when I am weak, then I am strong" - (in God's power!) [2 Cor. 12:10]

Third, and simply as one example of the multitude of more common and contemporary folks whose life has been allowed to suffer in some very manifest way- Joni Eareckson Tada:

Joni has been consigned to a wheelchair as a quadriplegic now for 50 years following a diving injury at age 18. Joni, a strong Christian disciple has devoted her entire life to the gospel message and helping to provide free wheelchairs to the physically disabled throughout the world. Joni has prayed many, many times for healing for herself. Despite not receiving physical healing (like Job, Paul and so many others) Joni has con¬tinued to serve God mightily.

While our God had unlimited power to grant physical healing in each and all of these cases, God chose not to protect Job from his suffering, nor remove Paul's thorn, nor allow Joni to stand and walk. While God can and does grant many, many physical healings He does not heal all - at least not physically during their earthly lives.

Understand that God's promise to heal all who ask in His name is fulfilled, but sometimes only and always ultimately in Act III {Heaven). However, God's promise of healing for all who ask is granted even in Act I for the most critical of all healings - namely spiritual healing, and the forgiveness of our sins.

Wilbur McCoy Otto

<u>Fifth</u>:	Evil sometimes drives man to God out of desperation or due to evil's unbearable consequences; also, once evil is recognized as rebellion against God, the cost of evil becomes too high to accept.
<u>Sixth</u>:	Full appreciation of God's mercy, love, gift of salvation or forgiveness often requires seeing engaging in great evil or tribulation;
<u>Seventh</u>:	Evil provides opportunities for God to display His Love, Power, Works, Mercy and Grace (and, in return for man to express his great love for God!)
<u>Eighth</u>:	Know well, however, that God does not use evil to punish individuals;

Recall Jesus's words upon confronting the man blind from birth, when asked: "Who sinned- this man or his parents?"

Jesus responded: "Neither this man nor his parents sinned, but this happened so that the works of God might be displayed. We must all do the work of Him who sent us. Night is coming when no one can work. While I am in this world, I am the light of the world."[26]

Ninth: But for evil or sin entertained and acknowledged there can be no gift of forgiveness nor salvation.

Tenth: As Jesus taught: who will love God more, the one whose forgiven debt is small or the one whose forgiven debt is large? (Luke 7:47)

Eleventh: Given human nature, God (like many coaches) know that some men react better to the "stick," other to the "carrot."

Twelfth: God promises - "to work all things for good for those who love God are called according to His purpose;"[27]

Note carefully that this incredible and universal promise to over- come or compensate for acts of evil requires the important pre-qualification of loving God and being called according to His purposes.

Thirteenth: God refused to prevent the great evil of having His own sinless Son beaten and crucified - knowing that this act of evil would result in the greatest good in all of History, being the sinless/spotless sacrifice and atonement for all repentant sinners to be saved for all of Eternity and Act III.

So why does God not grant physical healing for all the faithful who ask during Act I? Some reasons are unknown, but some are known, including:

- to keep us weak and dependent on God's strength;
- to keep us trusting in God and His Grace;
- to enhance God's power;
- to keep us within God's Will throughout our lives;
- to preserve us for a time as examples for others- both the afflicted and the non-afflicted;
- to preserve and strengthen our humility and protect us from the weakness of boasting, thereby detracting from the power and grace of God;
- to enable the afflicted to provide comfort to others similarly afflicted as only they can;
- to serve as a reminder of the consequences of sin - as a result of mankind's sin in the Garden of Eden - "I will greatly increase your pains in childbearing." Gen. 3:16; and
- all in all, to aid greatly in achieving God's priority, a priority that needs to be ours, namely - "... seek first His Kingdom and His righteousness - and all these things shall be given to you as well." (Mt. 6:33).

26. Jo: 9:3
27. Ro 8:28

Also very helpful is Charles Stanley's comment regarding the "storms" of life.[28]

In addition, let's consider the following factors and circumstances that may help to explain God's purposes and the "work" of evil and pain in our lives:

First: We are not always able to know or appreciate what is "good" without first having seen evil. (The reverse may sometimes be true also, i.e., that one cannot always recognize evil without knowing good.)

Second: Evil often leads to much good - good that would otherwise never occur (e.g., charity in response to needs created by evil or disaster). Almost all of America's non -profit hospitals originated from Christian outreach in the face of illness, disaster or evil - much of this arising during the Civil War.

Third: Overcoming evil or trials helps to build perseverance, courage, discipline, obedience and character, just as fire transforms iron into steel.

Fourth: Evil confronting man - particularly man with a strong, free will presents man with a difficult choice-but when resisted can result in building integrity, sincerity, righteousness, courage, obedience, etc.

Fourteenth: If we accept that Heaven is forever - and by comparison that our life here on Earth is but the twinkling of the eye - or "a mist that appears for a little while"[29]-we can appreciate not only the significance of our roles on Life's stage during Act I or II, but the brevity of time we have which to achieve Life's primary purpose and Gods Plan.

Fifteenth: Finally, while we must not rely on it - it is comforting to know of the following promise of God (not unlike a U.S. President's right to Pardon):

"I will have mercy on whom I will have mercy, and I will have compassion on whom I will have compassion..."[30]

As such, we must have faith in God's ultimate power of mercy and com¬ passion and our Creator God's sovereign right to deal with His creatures in whatever manner He wishes. Those with whom God will consider granting such compassion and mercy will likely include:

- the unborn;
- infants and others who die young;
- those who die at the hands of evil; and
- any individual found deserving of extra-judicial mercy and com¬ passion in God's wisdom.

Note: We will only know of these acts of mercy if we ourselves receive God's gift of Salvation.

---

28.   God often allows "storms" to come into our lives for the following purposes, to: get our attention;
- eliminate or surrender sin in our life;
- conform us to Christ; equip us to do His will; add to our wisdom;
- strengthen our commitment to Christ;
- provide us with direction; and/or
- provide us with an anchor.

29.   Jas. 4-14

30.   Ex. 33:19

VIII. SOME INSIGHTS INTO GOD'S CONVERSION PROCESS

While God wishes all world actors to choose to love and obey God, and to adapt their lives to that of God's son whose mission in the World as Messiah included modeling proper behavior, views, actions, love, etc., God also wants, indeed requires man's choice to be free, independent and genuine. God could have created all men with a baked-in pre-destination; however, this would not only be un-holy and unjust, but it would also be meaningless and ineffective for God's purposes, including one's qualification for Heaven. God means for our life experiences to be character-building and life-changing, knowing that this almost always requires difficult tri¬ also, testing - even forging with fire. Of course, God also understands that given man's strong and independent free will by exposing an unsaved person to the temptations of evil, there will always be the risk of that person's permanent loss to evil.[31]

God knows well human psychology (no surprise - after all He is our Creator!). Once converted, disciples make great teachers and exemplars for life-change, who can then best inspire others to change their lives and/ or allow the Holy Spirit to renew their hearts. God knows that this pro¬cess will repeat itself one on one, with ever-multiplying effect. God seeks to utilize the powerful impact of personal, first-hand testimonies to have its persuasive effect in one-on-one situations. As such, God has designed a process of inspiration, belief, faith, regeneration and salvation of the human soul, changing one heart at a time, and over time. In God's unimpeachable wisdom He created and built into Life's Play a process that is very personal, sometimes instantaneous and at other times life-long in its formation or presentation, but always genuine, meaningful and effective.

God's Gift of Eternal Life

Note carefully, the law of gift-giving:

- A gift is given by the Donor to the Donee;
- The Donee must willingly accept or receive the gift;
- The gift is legally effective upon delivery by the Donor and receipt by the Donee;
- A gift once given cannot be revoked.

Gifts need to be contrasted with promises on condition wherein the prospective "donor" does not deliver a gift to the prospective "donee," but rath e r says either:

A) "If you perform satisfactorily - then I will deliver a gift"; this is a promise of gift on condition precedent; alternatively, a prospective donor may say-

B) "I will let you have temporary possession of this prospective 'gift' now, but if you do not perform satisfactorily, I will withdraw my' gift" '; this is a promise subject to condition subsequent.[32]

Neither of these latter promises represent God's gift of eternal life Any belief or teaching that God's gift of eternal life is a promise on condition, i.e., that it does not occur until the death of the Donee, or that the promise is made but can be revoked if God finds you have not performed to His satisfaction is a lie of Satan.

However, God's "gift" of eternal life is made only coincidental with a change of heart in the recipient, a change where is itself a gift of God - through the Holy Spirit - namely the spiritual gift of heart regeneration, or one' s being " born again." This act of God and the Holy Spirit requires no works, only the election of our free-will to seek repentance for our sinful self, acknowledging God and Messiah Christ as the Son of God, and accepting

---

31.   See I Cor. 10 :1 3 where God promised believers, "He will not let you be tempted beyond what you can bear."

32.   Heb 6:4 is not an example of the gift of life being given and then lost, but rather a gift offered and" tasted" but   never accepted or "swallowed.

His substitutionary crucifixion and death as our only means of reconciliation with and justification before God.

In further reference to God's gift of salvation and eternal life as a present and completed gift - note the following Scripture:

- "For it is by grace you have been saved, through faith ... and this not from yourselves, it is the gift of God - so that no one can boast." [Eph. 2:8-10]
- Jesus' reply to Nicodemus: " No one can see the Kingdom of God unless he is born again ... of the spirit." (By definition 'being born again" occurs at the very moment of being born again - a moment of time during one's life - not a moment at or after death.] (Jo 3:3]
- My sheep listen to my voice. I know they follow me. I give them eternal life and they shall never perish; no one can snatch them out of my hand nor out of my Father's hand. I and the Father are one. [Jo 10:27-30]
- "...The wages of sin is death, but the gift of God is Eternal Life..." (Ro 6:23] "Thanks be to God for his indescribable gift."[2Cor 9:15]
- "... that everyone who believes in Him (Son of God) may have [not get or acquire] eternal life."[Jo 3:15]
- "... whoever believes in him (Jesus, the Christ) shall not perish but have [not receive or acquire] eternal life." (Jo 3:16]
- ". . .that you may stand firm in all the will of God, mature and fully assured" (not just hopeful). [Col 4:12]
- Abraham received during his life that which God promised. (Heb 10:22]
- Job's possessions were doubly restored by God during Job's lifetime, in light of Job's faithfulness. (See Job 42:10]

Finally, God, our creator - and the creator of all practicality, human psychology, and love - knows well that His graceful act of giving to sinful man the most unimaginable gift of love for Eternity, together with the Holy Spirit, will cause a unique and authentic humbling, and create within man a new nature and compelling need - all in the image of God - to express genuine acts of love and obedience on behalf of God. Contrast this evolutionary change to the situation where a gift is promised - e.g.by parent to child - dependent on the child's performance, over a long period of time, being found satisfactory by the parent.

IX. THE NATIONS OF ISRAEL AND AMERICA

We know that God has chosen Abraham - along with the offspring Jewish people and Nations through which He is telling His Story, allowing His Plan to unfold, and His purposes to be dis¬ played for all the World. As such, God's Reality Play spotlights the people and nation Israel throughout the first 3,000 years of their history, including their exiles into Egypt and Babylon, and then after the Exodus, returning to their promised land, followed by the birth, crucifixion, death and RESURRECTION of Messiah-Christ and the destruction of Jerusalem's second Temple in 70 AD. Following these events came the great Dispersion of the Jewish peoples' and their homelessness and suffering the Holocaust over nearly 2,000 years between 70 AD, and May14, 1948[33] when a Nation-State of Israel was declared in Palestine.[34]

However, we submit that what cannot be disputed is God's over-arching intent and plan to turn the Jewish people to their Messiah-Christ rather than a return of the Jewish people to Nation status - but all the same, the latter may well serve as an important sign or symbol of the former.

---

33.   Gen. 22: 15-18:

The Lord said to Abraham -

"I swear by myself... because you have not withheld your son, your only son, I will surely bless you, and make your descendants as numerous as the stars in the sky, and as sand on the seashore... through your offspring all nations on earth will be blessed, because you obeyed me."

Gen. 18:18:

"Abraha m will surely become a great and powerful nation, and all nations on earth will be blessed through him. For I have chosen him, so that he will direct his children... to keep the way of the Lord, by doing what is right and just...".

Gen.12:2:

"I will make you into a great nation and I will bless you." RE:1948:

God used WWI, the Balfour Declaration and President Truman to bring about Israel's re-birth as a Nation. Truman - a most unlikely choice by Roosevelt (but not God) to be Roosevelt's Vice President - succeeded Roosevelt when God ordained him to die on April 12, 1945. Actingvirtuallyalmost unilaterally, and against the advice of his Secretary of Defense (Gen. George Marshall), his Secretary of State, and the United Nations, Truman wrote a handwritten note stating that the U.S. would recognize Israel as a Nation effec¬tive 5/r4 /48 - allowing Israelis' to return to their promised land. While Roosevelt had been anti-Israel as a Nation, God had dearly positioned Truman, a solid Christian and student of the Bible and Bible prophecy, together with one of Truman's closest friends - (pre-WWII, during WWII as soldiers, and after WWII as partners in a men's clothing store business in Kansas City) - one Eddie Jacobson, who happened to be a strong Zionist. (See Truman, by David McCullough, Simon & Shuster, 1992)

34.   Some contend that too much attention is paid to the re-birth of the Israel Nation in 1948, the recapture of Jerusalem in 1967 and the part played by the Nation of Israel in eschatological commentary, or in general.

It may well be that return of the Israeli people to at least part of the lands of Canaan promised by God to Abraham and his offspring is more symbolic that central to God's Plan for the end-times and the reign of Christ. Some may even argue that it is not at all a critical issue.

During the latter years of the Israeli Dispersion America made its formal appearance onto the world stage in 1787-89. From its beginnings, America for the most part has maintained a close and prayerful relationship with the Jewish people and their history. The evidence is strong that God has protected and blessed America so it could serve a key role in the worldwide spread of God's Plan and the Gospel message primarily over the years 1750 to the current time. One can well argue that as America blessed the Jewish people, God has blessed America by nurturing its creation, development and protection at critical moments throughout America's history.[35] However, we need to note that this Blessing and protection of America is not forever, but only so long as "America" loves and honors God and His commands, including the command to bless that which the people of Israel have brought to the World.

In this regard, note that while we as individuals often seek to identify with particular leaders, assigning to them favor or disfavor, God rarely does so. While God certainly uses certain individuals, whether of good or bad character, of lower or higher status to achieve His purposes,[36] it is primarily through the Jewish people that God's Plan and purposes have been displayed and fulfilled over time. Thus, allowing one or another individual to achieve worldly financial success or national leadership should never be equated with God's approval or disapproval of either that individual or nation. Of course, at the same time God extends His Blessings to His children every day, and in all manner of ways.

As we live our lives, we should all strive to be like Christ, who as God and Creator of all, is incapable of bias, prejudice, or preference when it comes to race, nationality, gender, community status or worldly distinction of any kind.[37] However, make no mistake that God certainly "favors" those disciples of Jesus who love, obey and serve Him - all integral to God's goals of advancing His Plan, displaying His Purposes for mankind, and ultimately His creation and population of Heaven.

---

35.   Gen.12:3:
        "I will bless those who bless you and curse those who curse you."
        God performed many "direct" miracles in giving rise to America - which while not a "Christian Nation" is a nation of peoples revering freedom of religion, founded in large part by people seeking who sought to express principles of the Judeo-Christian religion. Recall God's direct action in protecting George Washington's life at critical times, helping the Colonial Army to survive against a stronger foe in the Revolutionary War, assuring victories at Antietam and Gettysburg, the Battles of Normandy, Midway, etc.

36   Most notably, Abraham, but also many other individuals including, Mary, Moses, David, Paul, et al. All are rare exceptions for us to model, although even with each of these individuals God imposed certain limita-tions, discipline, etc.

37   "There is neither Jew nor Gentile, slave nor free male nor female since with God and the Church, made up of regenerated hearts there can be no prejudice."

X. FINAL NOTES

What Triggered This Little Book?

The central theme of this book is to illustrate the over-arching love of our Great Creator God - and to reach out to all families and individuals who have suffered or experienced severe tragedy of one form or another in their lives - in an effort to illustrate that God does and will not aban¬ don them.

The following examples of a few diverse tragedies will suffice:

- while backing his car out of the family driveway, a father runs over and kills or severely injures his only child;
- a teenage girl reaches out to help a troubled teen-friend and dies when the "friend" plunges a sword into her in the backyard of her home;
- a young woman becomes paralyzed in an accident; the suicide of a loved one;
- victims of the Holocaust; or
- victims of wars, genocides, natural disasters, diseases, etc. etc.

In reaching out we attempt to respond with the following questions - asked not only by each of the above, but millions of others, and perhaps all of us at one time or another during Life's Play:

a: "How could, why would, God allow such a horrible, evil thing to happen?"

a: " Is God not loving? Is God not omnipotent?"

a: "I have been faithful to God; what is God's purpose - what is He saying to me in this tragedy?"

a: How can one possibly love such a God?

In response to all of these questions, we have offered all that has preceded. Additionally, our response requires an understanding of God's still developing World History , being played out in large part perhaps through the Nation Israel and the Mid-East - even if only symbolically but certainly through all of God's children through the World, including America - incidental to its role in the world-wide spread of the Gospel and growth of the Christian Church (presently wit¬ ness notably in China) - helping all to better understand God's plan of salvation and His grace and mercy offered to and all in a world so divided over superficialities.

It is our hope and prayer that both the responses to the above questions as well as God's Plan of Salvation and His purposes might be meaningfully, and forcefully presented when viewed through the perspective of God's "Life's Reality Play."[38]

We certainly need to under¬ stand that each of our lives are in fact real life dramas and part of a World Life drama in which every person ever born appears and lives his/her life on our World's stage of life and with each of us appearing only in one particular Scene of Act I or Act II in a Play that extends over some 5000 years or more. As such, your life not only has incredible and eternal meaning, but mean¬ ing to others, many of whom you will never know until Act III.

---

38.   Understand that any human effort to fully know or understand all the precise details and timings of God's plan is not only impossible, but in part has been forbidden by God. Nevertheless, for the sake of salvation and the Gospel broad outlines of what Scripture does reveal is being presented and offered.

As such, we need to all visualize our life as one being played out day-to-day - as it is, and at this very moment - on the World stage, all within the perspective and purpose of God's overall plan, with appreciation for all that has preceded and all that which is yet to come. Through this per¬spective, perhaps we can better see our lives as either aligned or misaligned with God's purposes and plan for each of us, and if necessary, allowing if not encouraging us to take whatever correc¬tive action may be necessary before the window into Heaven closes.

By The Way Just Who Is the Audience in God's Reality Play?

As one of the millions of actors appearing on stage in one Scene or another of a Play extending over a period of 5,000 years or more, you might well ask, "If all the people are on stage as actors, just who is the audience in Life 's Reality Play?"

The answer, of course, is the most important audience ever, namely, our Triune God - God the Father, God the Son-Messiah Jesus Christ - and the Holy Spirit, Comforter and Counselor, together with all of the Angels (and possibly the "Communion of Saints" to include maybe you!) who are within the "Company of Heaven" - all of whom will arise and heartily cheer when it comes time for each actor who is to re-appear on stage for Act III.

In this further connection, at the end of Act II, and just prior to the commencement of Act III, the Triune God will offer a critique of each actor who has ever appeared on stage by expressing to each actor individually (can you imagine this!) either of the following statements:

"Well done, my good and faithful Servant!" (Mt. 25:23]

-or-

"Depart from me, I never knew You."[Mt. 25:41)

The End (though not for all!)

About The Author

The Lord is the "Author" of all that is accurate and true, the rest is the author's.

Wilbur McCoy "Joe" Otto is a graduate of Dickinson College (BA with Honors in Economics) and the University of Michigan Law School (JD) and the Judge Advocate General's School, Charlottesville, Virginia, with Honors. He was commissioned an officer in the US Regular Army, Judge Advocate Generals Corps, and appointed as Assistant Professor of Law at the US Military Academy at West Point, New York 1961-65. While at the Academy, Captain Otto was asked to revise the Academy's Regulations, and having recently had two daughters born at West Point, he recommended open¬ ing the Academy to women candidates, which was approved and implemented by the Department of the Army in 1973 and adopted by all the military academies thereafter. Kiera, the daughter of our first daughter Christian joined he Class of 2024 at West Point in June 2020.

Mr. Otto served as assistant Professor of Economics at Point Park University and Assistant Professor of Health Law at the University of Pittsburgh's School of Health and Rehabilitation Sciences for many years. He has served as a faculty member of Trial Advocacy Institutes at the law schools of the University of Michigan, University of Pittsburgh, and Duquesne University, and, for the Pennsylvania Trial Lawyers Association and PA Bar Institute. He is recognized as the first trial lawyer in the United States to utilize video testimony in both state and federal court rooms in 1969 and 1970. Mr. Otto is also recognized as one of the first lawyers to help Universities and Medical centers create off-shore captive insurance programs at great cost-savings to our University Medical Centers.

A trial lawyer for over fifty years, Mr. Otto is a former CEO of the largest trial/litigation firm in Pittsburgh, Pennsylvania having helped to build the firm to 200 from 10 members when he first joined and is presently the principal of Otto Law Group, LLC. He is a past president of the Academy of Trial Lawyers of Allegheny County and is a Fellow of the International Society of Barristers and the American Bar Foundation. Mr. Otto is a member of the Pennsylvania, District of Columbia and the U.S. Supreme Courts.

Finally, and most importantly, Mr. Otto, a longtime student of the Bible and biblical history and Sunday school teacher is the husband of Nancy Ann (Fox) Otto for 63 years, the father of four children (all lawyers, and Christian judge), father-in-law to three more lawyers and grandfather of nine wonderful grandchildren.

The eldest grandchild, Joshua, is a graduate of the U.S. Naval Academy at Annapolis (marrying a class¬ mate, Jordan), and who along with granddaughter, Kiera, is carrying on the family's unbro¬ken record of military service to America including the Revolutionary War (Ben Franklin's brother, John), the Civil War (Will's father, William, who died at the Battle of Chickamauga.), WWI (Will's son, MacDonald, who gave his life in the Influenza Pandemic of 1918), WWII (Charles Fox,) the Korean War (brother Richard, Purple Heart) and Joe at West point driving the Viet Nam War and son Mark during The Lebanon/Middle East Crisis (son, Mark).

Index

A
Abel
Abortions
Abraham
Acre Action Acts
Adirondacks
Agnostic Africanus America
Ananias
Ancient Document(s)
Andrew
Angel
Anno Domino
Answers
Antiquities of the Jews
Apocryphal
Apostles
Appearance(s)
Aristotle
Ascension
Assyrians
Asphyxiation
Atheistic
Atonement
Augustine

B
Babylon
Bankruptcy
Baptism
Bartholomew
Battery Park Belief
Believers
Bethlehem Bias
Bible
Blood
Bones

Born again
Born to die
Boston Strangler
Bribed
Brick(s)
Buddha
Buettner, Dennett
Burden of Proof
Burial
Business Record

C
Caesar
Cahn, Jonathan
Cain
Calendar
Capital
Capital Hill
Carbon 14 List
Catalogue of Fishes Cedar(s)
Centrality
Change
Charismatic
Child of God
Children Christ
Christianity
Chronology
Church(es)
Cicero
Cloth(s)
Coagulation
Codex Sinaiticus
Codex Vaticanus
Colson
Commission Commodus
Communion

Compassion
Confucius
Congress
Conscience
Consequence
Constantine
Conversion
Corinthians
Covenant
Created
Creeds
Crisis/Crises
Critic
Cross
Crucifixion
Curse
Curtain

D
Damascus
Dark/Darkening
Daschle
Dating
David
DaVinci
Dead Sea Scroll
Death
Declaration(s)
Demons
DeSalvo, Albert
Deuteronomy
Diner
Disciples
DNA
Doers of evil
Donkey Dream

Dunn, James
Dying

E
Einstein, Albert
Emmaus
Empty
Enemy
Environment(al)
Ephesians
Equality
Erasmus
Escape
Essenes
Eternity
Eusebius
Events
Evergreen
Evidence
Evil
Exclusivity
Excruciating
Exemplary
Exodus
Eyewitness
Ezekiel
Ezra

F
Facts
Feast [of un-leav- ened bread]
Federal Hall
Female
Fertile
Fig (trees)
Financial [interest]
Finished
Fire
First
Fish(es)
Fisherman
Five Hundred (500)
Flesh
Flood
Folded
Foreign (citizens)
Forgiveness

Free
Free Will
Freedom
Freedom Tower
French (Revolution)
Fruit [fruitful]

G
Gabriel
Galatians
Galilee
Genesis
Geneva Bible
Gifts [of God]
God Gospel(s)
Grace
Grandchildren
Granite
Grapes
Great Britain
Great Commission
Greek
Greenleaf, Simon
Ground Zero
Guards
Guest, John
Guttenberg, Johann

H
Hagar
Halieutica
Hallucinations
Hammurabi
Harbinger
Heart
Heaven
Hebrew
Henry VIII
Herod
Historians
History
Hitchcock, Mark
Hitler
Holy
Holy Spirit
Hope (Tree of)
Hospital Human Hypovolemia

I
Idol
Illusions
Important
Inaugural
Inequality
Inspired/Inspiration
Intellect
Irenaeus
Isaac Ishmael
ISIS
Israel

J
James, brother of Jesus
James, son of Zebedee
James, Alphaeus Jamnia
Jefferson, Thomas
Jeremiah
Jerome
Jerusalem
Jesus
Jew
John
Joseph (of Arimethea)
Josephus
Judas Jude Jurors
Justification

K
Kant
Kennedy
Kill
King
King James

L
Lapse
Lazarus
Letters
Leviticus
Lewis, C. S
Life
Limbaugh, Stephen
Lincoln, Abraham
Lives
Lord

Ltidemann, Gerd
Lunatic
Luther, Martin

M
Male Manchester, VT
Mark
Martyr, Justin
Mary
Mary Magdalene
Materialism
Matthew
Matthias
Medical
Mediterranean
Mercy
Messiah
Metherell, Alex
Middle-East
Military Miracle(s)
Mist
Moses
Muhammad
Muslim(s)

N
Name(s)
Napkin
Nature
Nero
N.Y. Stock Exchange
New Testament [NT]
Niccodemus
Nicea
Noah
NIV

O
Octavius
Official Document
Old Testament [OT]
One Third
Oppian
Origen

P
Pain
Palmer, Steve
Panel
Paradise
Past Recollections Recorded
Patrick Paul
Payne, J. Barton
Peace
Peter
Phillip
Physician
Psalms(s)
Picknett
Pilate/Pilatus,
Pontius
Pilgrims
Plato
Pliny, The Younger
Pluralism
Polycarp
Pompey
Pornography
Post-Resurrection
Prayer
Prejudice
Pre-Resurrection Preparation, day of
Prince, Clive Prophecy(ies) Protection
Prune Puritans Purpose

Q
Qu'ran
Questions(s)
Qumran

R
Rainbow
Ram
Rapture
Re-birth
Recordings
Record(s)
Red Cross
Redemption
Reformation
Regeneration(ed)

Religion
Report(s)
ResGestae
Resurrection
Revelation
Rodgers, John
Roman(s)

S
Sabbath
Sacrifice
Safe
Safety
Salome
Salvation
Salvation Army
Samuel
Sarah
Satan Saul
Science Scribe(s)
Scriptural
Sea (of Galilee)
Secular
Senate Majority Leader
Septuagint
Seven (7)
Severus
Shroud
Sidon
Silver
Simon
Skeptics
Slave
Smith
Socrates
Solomon
Soul
Spices
Spirit
Spiritual
Spring
Sproul
St. Paul's Chapel
Stephen
Stock Market
Stone

Stoner, Peter
Stott, John
Stratagem
Strobel, Lee
Struggle
Study
Substitution(ary)
Sunday
Sword
Sycamore
Symbol

T
Tacitus, Cornelius
Tax Collector
Temple
Ten Commandments
Testimony
Texas
Thalus
Theodosius
Thessalonians
Third
Thirst
Thomas
Thorn
Time
Timothy
Titus
Toledoth Jesu
Tomb Transplant
Tranquillus, Suetonius
Treasure
Tree
Tree of Hope Trial (s)
Tribulations
Trinity
Trust
Truth
Turin
Twin Towers
Tyndale, William
Tyre

U
U.S. Congress

U.S. Constitution
U.S. Senate Majority Leader

V
Virgin birth
Virgin Mary

W
Washington, George
Warning [of 9/II]
Way(s)
West Point
Will
Wisdom
Wise
Women
Word
World
World Vision
Wycliffe, William

X

Y
Years

Z
Zechariah
Zimmerman,Mark

www.ingramcontent.com/pod-product-compliance
Lightning Source LLC
Chambersburg PA
CBHW080844120626
46553CB00009B/2559